Amigurumi Friends

Amigurumi Friends

CILLA WEBB

NEW HOLLAND

First published in 2014 by
New Holland Publishers
London • Sydney • Cape Town • Auckland
www.newhollandpublishers.com

The Chandlery Unit 114 50 Westminster Bridge Road London SE1 7QY
1/66 Gibbes Street Chatswood NSW 2067 Australia
Wembley Square First Floor Solan Road Gardens Cape Town 8001 South Africa
218 Lake Road Northcote Auckland New Zealand

A catalogue record of this book is available at the British Library and at the National Library of
Australia

ISBN: 9781780094564

10 9 8 7 6 5 4 3 2 1

Publisher: Fiona Schultz
Project editor: Simona Hill
Designer: Tracy Loughlin
Stylist: Sue Stubbs
Photographer: Sue Stubbs
Production director: Olga Dementiev
Printer: Toppan Leefung Printing Limited

Follow New Holland Publishers on
Facebook: www.facebook.com/NewHollandPublishers

Contents

Introduction

I first learnt to knit when I was a little girl and loved to make clothes for my teddies. When I became a mum, I knitted soft toys for my baby and soon began to design my own. My eldest son, then two, provided the inspiration for this book. He loved to dress and undress his soft toys. He often got quite frustrated though, when he discovered some teddy bears had their clothes sewn on. While writing (or knitting) this book I wanted to design toys that would appeal to every child and most importantly could be dressed and redressed in different outfits. All these little critters are made to the same dimensions and so their clothes are interchangeable.

Let me introduce you to the characters in this book: First there is Master Giraffe, who is passionate about martial arts and enjoys working out on his exercise mat. Another fitness fanatic is Master Teddy who loves to go for a run in his snazzy jogging suit and matching trainers. Master Monkey loves to dress up and spends most of his free time fighting crime as his alter ego Super Monkey! Master Wabbit is busy all year round working in Santa's workshop, however, his favourite time of year is when he gets to go on sleigh rides with SC himself! A more laid back kind of character is Master Woof. He is nicely dressed in his cosy winter outfit and enjoys lounging around with his knitted friends. Miss Fox prefers spring over winter. You'll usually find her tending her garden in her wellington boots. Miss Mouse, on the other hand, prefers the glamorous lifestyle and enjoys wearing her best outfit to go to fancy tea parties. Miss Puss loves spending sunny summer days on the beach where she can splash around to her heart's content. Miss Sheep is all set for the new school year and is happy to be learning lots of exciting new skills. Finally, Miss Squirrel is ready to crawl into a warm and comfy bed with her soft toy and snuggly hot water bottle.

As you can see, there's something to knit for every child in your life so why not pick up your needles and get started! Ready, Set... hold on, let's check the essentials first.

Supplies

YARN
All my little critters have been knitted using Wendy Merino DK (8-ply) wool, which is soft, durable and most importantly washable! When choosing the yarn for your new bundle of friends, you could opt for lighter or heavier yarn weights, though keep in mind that this will make your critter smaller or bigger than my intended size.

NEEDLES
All my creatures have been knitted using 3.5 mm (US 4) straight needles, which is smaller than suggested on the yarn band. This allows for the finished fabric to be firm and not show too much of the stuffing.

TOY STUFFING
As with the yarn, choose a stuffing that is washable and suitable for soft toys.

ACCESSORIES
A tapestry needle, a sewing needle, black thread for the eye lashes and a pair of scissors are essential.

SMALL BUTTONS
Some of the accessories and clothes require small buttons. However, if you are creating these toys for a small child, who might possible chew or swallow them, then just substitute the buttons for some fancy embroidery stitches instead so your toy does not become a safety hazard.

Abbreviations

[ ] x times: Knit the instructions between the brackets x amount of times.

*; rep from * to end: Repeat the instructions between the * and ; until the end of the row.

Beg: Beginning.

K: Knit, if followed by a number, knit that amount of stitches.

K2tog: Knit two stitches together knitwise.

Kfb: Knit in the front and back of the stitch, creating an increase.

P: Purl.

G st: Garter stitch: knit every row.

P2tog: Purl two stitches together purlwise.

Pfb: Purl in the front and back of the stitch, creating an increase.

Psso: Pass slipped stitch over.

Rem: Remaining.

Skpo: Slip 1, knit 1, pass slipped stitch over

Sl1: Slip one stitch to the right-hand needle

Ssk: Slip 1, slip 1, knit these two slipped stitches together through the back, creating a decrease.

St(s): Stitch(es).

St st: Stocking stitch: alternate a row of knitting and a row of purling.

Yo: yarn over: wrap the yarn over the right-hand needle.

Safety first

Anyone dealing with children will know they like to figure out the ins and outs of their toys and usually end up chomping on parts or pulling things apart. Ensure that all parts are securely attached and that your knitted fabric has a tight gauge so little people cannot pull the stuffing out.

Sewing up

For a clean edge I prefer to use the mattress stitch when sewing finished pieces together.

To join two pieces vertically place both your pieces side by side with the right side facing up. Insert your tapestry needles under the horizontal bar between the first two stitches on the left side and repeat on the right. Continue going back and forth until you've worked your way up to the top. Pull the yarn tight and watch the seam disappear as if by magic!

When joining two pieces horizontally (e.g. the cast-on or cast-off edge) insert the needle under the V point of the first stitch on one side and repeat on the other side. Work all the way across the seam and pull the yarn tight.

Casting on

There are many different ways of casting on yarn: however, when it comes to toy knitting, I find the cable cast on gives an attractive and even edge. Here's how to do it:

Start by making a slip knot on the left-hand needle. Place the right-hand needle behind the first stitch and loop the yarn around it. Pull the loop over and onto the left-hand needle. Now insert the needle between the first and second stitch and loop the yarn over. Pull the next stitch onto the left-hand needle and repeat until the desired number of stitches are cast on.

Knitting

Starting with your stitches on the left-hand needle and the yarn behind the work, insert the tip of the right-hand needle in the front of the first stitch. Wrap the yarn around your needle counter clockwise and pull the loop through the first stitch, sliding the worked stitch off the left-hand needle and on to the right-hand one. Repeat this until all the stitches are on the right-hand needle. Swap the needles over and repeat. For a clean edge, simply slide the first stitch onto the right-hand needle without actually knitting it, then knit all the stitches to the end of the row.

Purling

This time start with the yarn in front, bring the tip of the right-hand needle through the back of the first stitch. Wrap the yarn counter clockwise around the tip of the needle and pull the loop through the back of the stitch. Slide the worked stitch off the left-hand needle and repeat. As with the knitted stitches, for a sharp edge simply slide the first stitch onto the right-hand needle without purling it.

KFB
(Knit in front and back of the stitch)
This stitch will allow you to increase your stitch count by 1. To do this knit the stitch but do not slip the worked stitch off the left-hand needle. Instead, insert the tip of the right knitting needle behind the left knitting needle and through the back of the same stitch. Knit the stitch again in the back and then slip the worked stitch off the needle. You should now have 2 stitches instead of 1.

PFB
(Purl in front and back of the stitch)
As before, however this time you're increasing on the purl side. Purl the stitch but do not slide the stitch from the left-hand needle. Instead, insert the tip of the right-hand needle in the back of the worked stitch and purl again. Slip the worked stitch off the left-hand needle.

K2tog
(Knit two stitches together)
This stitch will decrease your stitch count by 1. To do this insert the tip of the right-hand needle through the next two stitches on the left knitting needle as if to knit. Work with these stitches as if they are one and knit as usual through the front loop of both at the same time.

P2tog
(Purl two stitches together)
This stitch creates a decrease. Insert the tip of the right-hand needle through the front of the next two stitches on the left-hand needle at the same time and purl them together as if they are one stitch.

Cast off (bind off)

Once you've reached the desired number of rows it's time to cast off. To do this, knit (or purl if you're on the wrong side of your work) the first two stitches, then insert the left-hand needle into the first stitch on the right-hand needle and pull this stitch up and over the second stitch you just knitted (or purled). Knit (or purl) the next stitch and repeat this process until only one stitch remains. Cut the yarn and draw the yarn end through the last stitch and fasten tightly.

Blocking

Sometimes when you've knitted a piece you might find it curls up slightly or, if it has eyelets, it might look scrunched up. Don't despair... there's a very simple solution to this. You must block your knitting. To do this you must pin the piece on a flat surface (I prefer to use the ironing board) and then either steam it gently (but ONLY if you're using acrylic) or make the fabric wet (if using wool). Every yarn is different and blocking instructions are often stated on the yarn band so make sure you follow them accurately.

Weaving in loose ends

Once you've blocked your piece it's time to get rid of those loose yarn ends. Use a tapestry needle to weave each strand through four or five stitches on the back of the work and then cut the left over yarn.

Changing colour

To change colour, simply start your row as you would normally. Insert your right-hand needle into the first stitch of the left-hand needle and wrap the first colour around. Then also loop your new colour around the needle and knit your first stitch. For the second stitch, insert your needle into the stitch, but this time only use the new colour to knit by wrapping the yarn and the tail end around the needle and knit. Repeat this last step twice more to ensure the yarn is secured.

Stranded knitting

For a few of these projects you'll need to master stranded knitting. Don't worry, it's not as hard as it seems. You simply follow the chart and add new colours when needed. However, you do have to make sure that you carry both (or more) yarns along until you reach the end of your row or pattern. You do this so that you can use them whenever you need them. To make sure your strands of yarn that have been carried along the back don't get too long twist them with your main yarn colour every four stitches. Try not to twist them in the same place on every row or you'll end up with a noticeable line in your knitted fabric. Also try to remember... it's always better to have slightly loose threads floating across the back of the work than tight ones.

Projects

Master Geoffrey Giraffe

Master Geoffrey Giraffe is a cheerful little chap who is obsessed with martial arts. He'll karate chop his way through breakfast and perform kicks for anyone who's interested. Why not knit one as a present for someone who's just starting out with this demanding sport, or as a reward for an achievement?

You will need

1 x 50 g (2 oz) ball Wendy Merino DK, Spice (DK, 100 per cent merino wool, 116 m per ball)

1 x 50 g (2 oz) ball Wendy Merino DK, Crepe (DK, 100 per cent merino wool, 116 m per ball)

2 x 50 g (2 oz) balls Wendy Merino DK, Cloud Dancer (DK, 100 per cent merino wool, 116 m per ball)

25 g (1 oz) Wendy Merino DK, Mulberry (DK, 100 per cent merino wool, 116 m per ball)

10 g (½ oz) Wendy Merino DK, Jet (DK, 100 per cent merino wool, 116 m per ball)

3.5 mm (US 4) knitting needles

Toy stuffing

Wood needle

LEGS

(Make 2, worked from bottom of foot.)
With Spice, cast on 22 sts.
Row 1 and all odd rows: Purl.
Row 2: K1, [kfb] 20 times, k1. 42 sts
Rows 3–17: Work in st st for 15 rows.
Row 18: K7, [k2tog] 14 times, k7. 28 sts
Row 20: K7, [k2tog] 7 times, k7. 21 sts
Rows 21–22: Change to Crepe and work 2 rows st st.
Rows 23–49: Following the chart below, work in st st for 27 rows, repeating the pattern across the row: On odd rows the last st is p1. On even rows the last st is k1.

Row 50: With Crepe, K4, [k2tog] twice, k5, [k2tog] twice, k4. 17 sts
Cast off loosely. Sew up the bottom of the foot first and continue along the back edge, leaving the cast-off edge open. Stuff firmly.

ARMS

(Make 2, work from top of arm.)
With Crepe, cast on 8 sts.
Row 1: Kfb, k to end. 9 sts
Row 2: Pfb, p to end. 10 sts
Rows 3–4: Rep last 2 rows. 12 sts
Rows 5–6: Cast on 2 sts, work to end. 16 sts
Rows 7–26: Join in Spice, work in st st for 20 rows, repeating the pattern given for the legs, across the row. Repeat the chart 4 times. Break off Crepe.
Row 27–32: Continuing in Spice, work 6 rows st st.
Row 33: Purl.
Row 34: [P1, p2tog] 5 times, p1. 11 sts
Row 35: [K2tog] 5 times, k1. 6 sts

18

Break off yarn and draw yarn through rem sts, pull tight and fasten. Sew along the top of the hand and side of the arm. Leave the cast-on edge open. Stuff firmly.

BODY
(Make 1, starting at neck.)
With Crepe, cast on 16 sts.
Rows 1–2: Work in st st for 2 rows.
Row 3: K1, [kfb] 14 times, k1. 30 sts
Rows 4–8: Work in st st for 5 rows.
Row 9: K1, [kfb] 28 times, k1. 58 sts
Rows 10–36: Work in st st for 27 rows.
Row 37: K1, [k2tog] 28 times, k1. 30 sts
Rows 38–42: Work in st st for 5 rows.
Row 43: K1, [k2tog] 14 times, k1. 16 sts
Break off yarn and draw yarn end through rem sts, pull tight and fasten. Sew up along the side edge using mattress st and stuff when three-quarters stitched. Continue to the cast-on edge, then draw the yarn through the cast-on edge and pull tight. Fasten and secure any loose threads. Stitch arms and legs to the body using mattress stitch.

HEAD
With Crepe, cast on 15 sts.
Row 1–2: St st 2 rows.
Row 3: K1, [kfb] 13 times, k1. 28 sts
Row 5: K1, [kfb, k1] 13 times, k1. 41 sts
Rows 6–18: Join in Spice and work in st st for 13 rows following pattern and repeating it 10 times across the row, finishing with a k1 for odd rows and p1 for even rows. Break off Spice.
Row 19: Continue in Crepe only, K1, *k1, kfb, k2; rep from * to end. 51 sts
Row 20–32: St st 13 rows.
Row 33: *K1, k2tog; rep from * to end. 34 sts
Row 35: *K2tog; rep from * to end. 17 sts
Row 36: P1, *p2tog; rep from * to end. 9 sts
Break yarn and draw tail through rem sts. Pull tight and sew along the edge. Stuff and leave a gap to add facial features before closing up.

To make the eyes, using Jet embroider three lines of satin stitch at row 19 (where you worked only in Crepe). Repeat on the other side of the head. Add a smile using running stitch, then work back along the line of stitching to fill in the gaps.

NECK
Cast on 16 sts in Crepe
Row 1: Knit.
Row 2–13: Work pattern for 13 rows.
Cast off and sew up along the edge. Stuff and use the neck to join the body to the head.

EARS
(Make 2.)
Cast on 12 sts in Crepe.
Row 1: K1, kfb, k2, kfb, k2, kfb, k2, kfb, k1. 16 sts
Row 2 and all even rows: Purl.
Row 3: K1, kfb, k4, kfb, k2, kfb, k4, kfb, k1. 20 sts
Row 4–6: St st 3 rows.
Row 7: K1, k2tog, k4, k2tog, k2, k2tog, k4, k2tog, k1. 16 sts
Row 9: K1, k2tog, k2, k2tog, k2, k2tog, k2, k2tog, k1. 12 sts
Row 11: K1, [k2tog] twice, k2, [k2tog] twice, k1. 8 sts
Row 13: K1, k2tog, k2, k2tog, k1. 6 sts
Row 15: K1, [k2tog] twice, k1.
Cast off. Fold the ears in half and sew along the edge. There is no need to stuff the ears. Attach to each side of the head.

HORNS
(Make 2.)
Using Spice, cast on 8 sts.
Row 1–4: St st 4 rows.
Row 5: [K1, kfb] 4 times. 12 sts.
Row 6: Purl.
Row 7: [K1, k2tog] 4 times. 8 sts
Row 8: *P2tog; rep from * to end. 4 sts.
Break off yarn and thread yarn end through rem sts. Sew along the side. Attach to the top of the head.

OUTFIT

TROUSERS

Starting from the bottom of the leg, cast on 30 sts in Cloud Dancer.

Row 1–28: St st 28 rows. Leave the stitches on a spare needle. Make a second identical piece.

Row 29: K30 then pick up and k the 30 sts from the spare needle. 60 sts.

Row 30–44: St st 15 rows.

Cast off and sew along the inside and back of the trousers.

TOP

Starting from the bottom, cast on 88 sts in Cloud Dancer.

Row 1: Skpo, k to the last 2 sts, k2tog. 86 sts

Row 2: Purl.

Row 3–28: Repeat [row 1 and 2] 13 times. 60 sts

Row 29: Skpo, k11, cast off 4 sts, k26, cast off 4 sts, k11, k2tog.

Work on the left 12 sts as follows:

Row 30 and all even rows: Purl.

Row 31: [K2tog] twice, k6, k2tog. 9 sts

Row 33: [K2tog] twice, k3, k2tog. 6 sts

Row 34–38: St st 5 rows.

Row 39: K4, k2tog. 5 sts

Cast off.

Join yarn to the middle 26 sts and work as follows:

Row 30: P.

Row 31: [K2tog] twice, k18, [k2tog] twice. 22 sts

Row 33: [K2tog] twice, k14, [k2tog] twice. 18 sts

Row 34–38: St st 5 rows.

Row 39: K2tog, k14, k2tog. 16 sts

Row 40: K5, cast off 6 sts, k5.

Row 41: Knit the first 5 sts only.

Cast off the remaining sts.

Join yarn to the 5 sts and repeat row 41, then cast off.

Join yarn to the 12 sts remaining and work as follows:

Row 30: Purl.

Row 31: Skpo, k6, [k2tog] twice. 9 sts

Row 33: Skpo, k3, [k2tog] twice. 6 sts

Row 34–38: St st 5 rows.
Row 39: Skpo, k4. 5 sts
Cast off and sew the shoulder seams together.

SLEEVES
(Make 2.)
Starting from the bottom of the sleeve, cast on 21 sts in Cloud Dancer.
Row 1–18: St st 18 rows.
Row 19–24: Cast off 3 sts at the beginning of the next 6 rows and work to the end. 3 sts
Cast off. Sew up the side edge of the sleeves and attach to the armholes.

BELT
Using Jet, cast on 100 sts.
Row 1–2: Garter st 2 rows.
Cast off.
Tie the belt around the giraffe and attach to the side of the top with a few stitches. This will ensure the belt doesn't get lost or become a safety hazard.

TRAINING MAT
Using Mulberry, cast on 21 sts.
Row 1: Knit.
Row 2: K5, *p3, k5; rep from * to end.
Row 3: P5, *k3, p5; rep from * to end.
Row 4: K5, *p3, k5; rep from * to end.
Row 5: K.
Row 6: K1, p3, *k5, p3; rep from * to last st, k1.
Row 7: P1, k3, *p5, k3; rep from * to last st, k1.
Row 8: K1, p3, *k5, p3; rep from * to last st, k1.
Row 9–32: Repeat rows 1–8. Cast off.

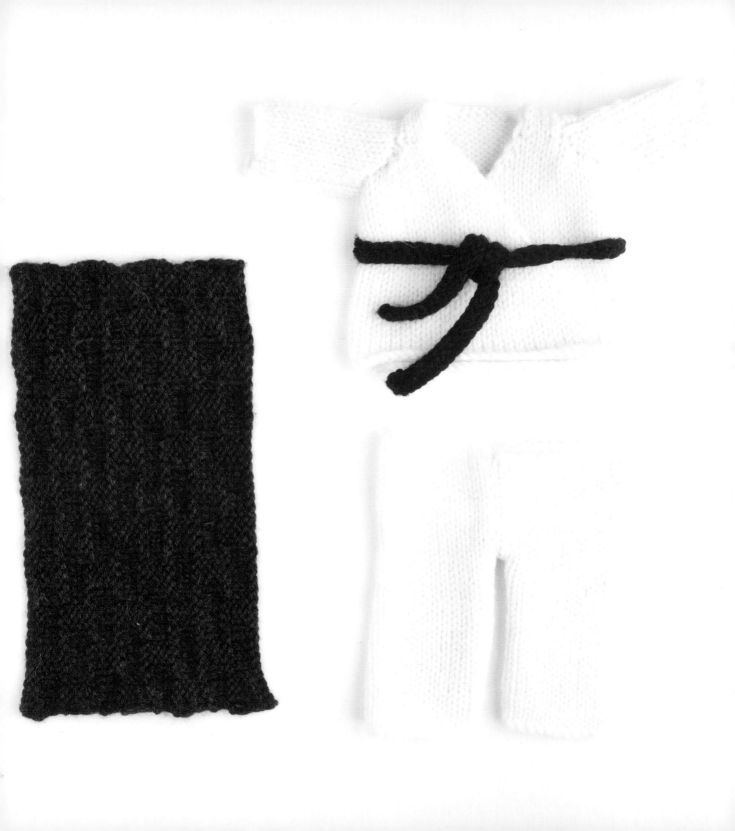

Master Maurice Monkey

Children love to dress up in superhero outfits and let their imagination run riot. Master Maurice Monkey, aka Super Monkey is an average primate during the day and a crime-stopping superhero at night. This little chap loves to swing in trees and protect the innocent but only when there are no bananas around!

You will need

2 x 50 g (2 oz) balls Wendy Merino DK, Spice (DK, 100 per cent merino wool, 116 m per ball)

1 x 50 g (2 oz) ball Wendy Merino DK, Wind Chime (DK, 100 per cent merino wool, 116 m per ball)

1 x 50 g (2 oz) ball Wendy Merino DK, Persian Red (DK, 100 per cent merino wool, 116 m per ball)

1 x 50 g (2 oz) ball Wendy Merino DK, Cadet (blue) (DK, 100 per cent merino wool, 116 m per ball)

Small amount of Maize and Jet yarn for the features

3.5 mm (US 4) knitting needles

Toy stuffing

Wool needle

Pins

LEGS
(Make 2, worked from bottom of foot.)
With Wind Chime, cast on 22 sts.
Row 1 and all odd rows: Purl.
Row 2: K1, [kfb] 20 times, k1. 42 sts
Rows 3–17: Work in st st for 15 rows.
Row 18: K7, [k2tog] 14 times, k7. 28 sts
Row 20: K7, [k2tog] 7 times, k7. 21 sts
Rows 21–49: Change to Spice and work in st st for 29 rows.
Row 50: K4, [k2tog] twice, k5, [k2tog] twice, k4. 17 sts
Cast off loosely. Sew up the bottom of the foot first and continue along the back edge, leaving the cast-off edge open. Stuff firmly.

RIGHT ARM
Starting from the top of the arm, cast on 8 sts in Spice.
Row 1: Kfb1, k to the end. 9 sts
Row 2: Pfb1, p to the end. 10 sts
Row 3–4: Repeat the last 2 rows. 12 sts
Row 5–6: Cast on 2 sts at the beginning of the next 2 rows. 16 sts
Row 7–26: St st 20 rows.
Row 27–28: Change to Wind Chime and st st 2 rows.
Row 29: (Thumb) K4, cast on 8 sts and k to end. 24 sts
Row 30–32: St st 3 rows.

Finger 1
Row 33: Cast off 12, [kfb] 3 times, turn. 6 sts (setting the other sts aside)
Row 34–36: St st 3 rows.
Row 37: [K2tog] 3 times. 3 sts
Pull a needle through the 3 remaining sts and pull tight.

Finger 2
Join the yarn to the next 2 sts and knit as follows:
Row 33: Cast on 2 sts, k to end. 4 sts
Row 34: Cast on 2 sts, p to end. 4 sts
Row 35–36: St st 2 rows.
Row 37: [K2tog] 3 times. 3 sts
Pull a needle through the 3 remaining sts and pull tight.

Repeat finger 1, then cast off the remaining 4 sts.

LEFT ARM
Repeat as for right arm to row 28.
Row 29: K12, cast on 8 sts and k to end. 24 sts.
Row 30–32: St st 3 rows.

Finger 1
Row 33: Cast off 4, [kfb] 3 times, turn. 6 sts (setting the other sts aside)
Row 34–36: St st 3 rows.
Row 37: [K2tog] 3 times. 3 sts
Pull a needle through the 3 remaining sts and pull tight.

Finger 2
Join the yarn to the next 2 sts and knit as follows:
Row 33: Cast on 2 sts, k to end. 4 sts
Row 34: Cast on 2 sts, p to end. 4 sts
Row 35–36: Work 2 rows st st.
Row 37: [K2tog] 3 times. 3 sts
Pull a needle through the 3 remaining sts and pull tight.
Repeat finger 1, then cast off the remaining 12 sts.
     Fold the thumb and sew along the edge. Sew up the edge of each finger, then fold the palm of the hand toward the middle and attach the bottom of each finger to this. Sew up the side of the arm and stuff firmly.

BODY
Starting at the neck, cast on 16 sts using Spice.
Rows 1–2: Work in st st for 2 rows.
Row 3: K1, [kfb] 14 times, k1. 30 sts
Rows 4–8: Work in st st for 5 rows.
Row 9: K1, [kfb] 28 times, k1. 58 sts
Rows 10–36: Work in st st for 27 rows.
Row 37: K1, [k2tog] 28 times, k1. 30 sts
Rows 38–42: Work in st st for 5 rows.
Row 43: K1, [k2tog] 14 times, k1. 16 sts
Break yarn and draw tail through rem sts, pull tight and fasten. Sew along the side and stuff firmly then sew up the neck edge. Attach the arms and legs to the body.

HEAD

With Spice, cast on 15 sts.

Row 1–2: Work 2 rows st st.

Row 3: K1, [kfb] 13 times, k1. 28 sts

Row 4 and all even rows: Purl.

Row 5: K1, [kfb, k1] 13 times, k1. 41 sts

Rows 6–8: Work in st st for 3 rows.

Row 9: K1, [k1, kfb, k1] 13 times, k1. 54 sts

Rows 10–14: Work in st st for 5 rows.

Row 15: K1, [k1, kfb, k2] 13 times, k1. 67 sts

Rows 16–30: Work in st st for 15 rows.

Row 31: K10 [k2tog] 6 times, k21, [k2tog] 7 times, k10. 54 sts

Row 32–36: St st 5 rows.

Row 37: K5, [k2tog] 9 times, k8, [k2tog] 9 times, k5. 36 sts

Row 38: Change to Wind Chime and purl.

Row 39: K5, [k1, kfb] 5 times, k8, [k1, kfb] 4 times, k5. 45 sts

Row 40–42: St st 3 rows.

Row 43: K5, [k1, kfb, k1] 5 times, k8, [k1, kfb, k1] 4 times, k5. 54 sts

Row 44–46: St st 3 rows.

Row 47: K5, [k1, k2tog, k1] 5 times, k8, [k1, k2tog, k1] 4 times, k5. 45 sts

Row 49: K5, [k1, k2tog] 5 times, k8, [k1, k2tog] 4 times, k5. 36 sts

Row 51: K5, [k2tog] 5 times, k8, [k2tog] 4 times, k5. 27 sts

Row 53: K1, [k2tog] 13 times. 14 sts

Cast off.

Fold both ends of the cast-off edge toward the centre of the edge. Sew along the cast-off edge and up the side of the head. Leave the cast-on edge open to allow for stuffing and adding facial features. Attach the head to the top of the body.

For the nostrils, add a small back stitch to each side of the snout and add a semi-circle of back stitches to create a smile.

EYES.

Cast on 18 sts in Crepe.

Row 1–8: St st 8 rows using the eye chart below.

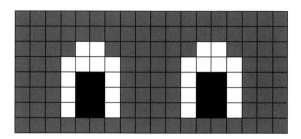

Row 9: K2tog, k5, k2tog and turn. Set aside the next 9 sts on a spare needle and continue to work on the right-hand 7 sts.

Row 10: P2tog, p3, p2tog. 5 sts

Row 11: K2tog, k1, k2tog. 3 sts.

Cast off.

Join yarn to the 9 sts set aside and repeat rows 9–11. Attach to the front of the monkey's head, just above the colour changes.

If need be, add a few back stitches along the outline of the pupil to tidy them up.

EARS

(Make 2.)

Cast on 22 sts in Crepe.

Row 1–6: St st 6 rows.

Row 7: K2tog, k7, [k2tog] twice, k7, k2tog. 18 sts

Row 8: Purl.

Row 9: K2tog, k5, [k2tog] twice, k5, k2tog. 14 sts

Row 10: P2tog, p3, [p2tog] twice, p3, p2tog. 10 sts

Break off yarn and thread yarn end through remaining stitches. Fold in half, sew up along the top and side edge and attach to each side of the head.

OUTFIT

ONESIE

Starting from the bottom of the leg, cast on 30 sts in Persian Red.

Rows 1–28: Work 28 rows st st. Leave the stitches on a spare needle and make a second identical piece.

Row 29: K30, then pick up and knit the 30 sts from the spare needle. 60 sts.

Row 30–34: St st 5 rows

Rows 35–38: Change to Cadet and work garter st for 4 rows.

Rows 39–54: Change to Persian Red and st st 16 rows, (AND AT THE SAME TIME commencing row 41, k22, work middle 16 sts from chart, k22).

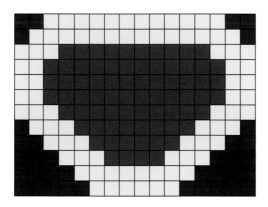

Row 55: K13, cast off 4, k26, cast off 4, k13.

Place the 13 first sts and the 26 middle sts on a holding needle. Join yarn to the remaining 13 sts purlwise and work as follows:

Row 56: Purl.

Row 57: [k2tog] twice, k9. 11 sts

Row 59: [k2tog] twice, k7. 9 sts

Row 60–63: St st 4 rows.

Row 64: Cast off 6 sts, p3. 3 sts

Row 65–66: St st 2 rows. Cast off.

Join yarn to the middle 26 sts purlwise and work as follows:

Row 56: [P2tog] twice, p to end. 24 sts

Row 57: [k2tog] twice, k to end. 22 sts

Row 58–59: Repeat row 56–57. 18 sts

Row 60–63: St st 4 rows.

Row 64: P4, cast off 10 sts, p4.

Rows 65–66: St st 2 rows.

Cast off.

Repeat row 64–66 for the 4 sts on the other side.

Join yarn to the last 13 sts waiting and work as follows:

Row 56: [P2tog] twice, p to end. 11 sts

Row 57: K.

Rows 58–59: Repeat rows 56–57. 9 sts

Rows 60–62: St st 3 rows.

Row 63: Cast off 6 sts, k3. 3 sts.

Rows 64–66: St st 3 rows.

Cast off.

SLEEVES

(Make 2.)

Starting from the cuff, cast on 20 sts in Persian Red.

Row 1: [Kfb, k1] 10 times. 30 sts

Rows 2–18: St st 17 rows.

Rows 19–24: Cast off 4 sts at the beginning of the next 6 rows and work to the end. 6 sts

Cast off. Using pins, fasten the back of the onesie and the inside of the leg. Sew along the inside of the legs and the back of the onesie. Join the tops of the shoulders. Sew up the side edge of the sleeves and attach to the armholes.

BOOTS

(Make 2.)

With Cadet, cast on 24 sts.

Row 1 and all odd rows: Purl.

Row 2: K1, [kfb] 22 times, k1. 46 sts

Rows 3–17: Work in st st for 15 rows.

Row 18: K8, [k2tog] 15 times, k8. 31 sts

Row 20: K7, [k2tog] 8 times, k8. 23 sts

Row 21–35: St st 15 rows.

Row 36: Cast off 7, k to end. 16 sts

Row 37: Cast off 7, p to end. 9 sts

Row 38: K2tog, k to last 2 sts, k2tog. 7 sts

Row 39: P2tog, p to last 2 sts, p2tog. 5 sts
Row 40: Repeat row 38. 3 sts
Cast off and sew along the bottom of the heel and up the side.

CAPE

Cast on 20 sts with Cadet.
Row 1: Kfb, k to the last st, kfb. 22 sts
Row 2 and all even rows: Purl.
Rows 3–8: [Repeat rows 1 and 2] 3 times. 28 sts
Row 9: Repeat row 1. 30 sts
Rows 10–12: St st 3 rows.
Row 13–24: [Repeat rows 9–12] 3 times. 36 sts
Row 25: Repeat row 1. 38 sts
Rows 26–32: St st 7 rows.
Row 33: Repeat row 1. 40 sts
Rows 34–44: St st 11 rows.
Row 45: Repeat row 1. 42 sts
Rows 46–50: St st 5 rows.

Cast off.
For best result block the cape prior to attaching it to the suit. Sew the cast-on edge to the back neckline of the onesie.

MASK

Using Cadet, cast on 56 sts.
Row 1: P.
Row 2: K21, cast off 6 sts, k2, cast of 6 sts, k21.
Rows 3–5: St st 3 rows on each section.
Row 6: K21, cast on 6 sts, k2, cast on 6 sts, k21. 56 sts
Row 7: Purl.
Cast off and sew up along the back edge.

Master Theodore Teddy

Do you happen to know any sport or fitness fanatics? Master Theodore Teddy would be their perfect companion. He wakes up at the crack of dawn to go out for a jog and still has plenty of energy to run laps around the block come night time. He is roaring to go in his trackswit and trainers.

Ready, set, KNIT!

You will need

1 x 50 g (2 oz) ball Wendy Merino DK, Funghi (DK, 100 per cent merino wool, 116 m per ball)

1 x 50 g (2 oz) ball Wendy Merino DK, Birch (DK, 100 per cent merino wool, 116 m per ball)

1 x 50 g (2 oz) ball Wendy Merino DK, Fennel (DK, 100 per cent merino wool, 116 m per ball)

1 x 50 g (2 oz) ball Wendy Merino DK, Pacific (DK, 100 per cent merino wool, 116 m per ball)

25 g (1 oz) Wendy Merino DK, Cloud Dancer (DK, 100 per cent merino wool, 116 m per ball)

Small amount of Jet (black) yarn

3.5 mm (US 4) knitting needles

Wool needle

Toy stuffing

Holding needle

Crochet hook

LEGS

(Make 2, worked from bottom of foot.)
With Funghi, cast on 22 sts.
Row 1 and all odd rows: Purl.
Row 2: K1, [kfb] 20 times, k1. 42 sts
Rows 3–17: Work in st st for 15 rows.
Row 18: K7, [k2tog] 14 times, k7. 28 sts
Row 20: K7, [k2tog] 7 times, k7. 21 sts
Rows 21–49: Work in st st for 29 rows.
Row 50: K4, [k2tog] twice, k5, [k2tog] twice, k4. 17 sts
Cast off loosely. Sew up the bottom of the foot first and continue along the back edge, leaving the cast-off edge open. Stuff and knit a second identical leg.

ARMS

(Make 2, work from top of arm.)
With Funghi, cast on 8 sts.
Row 1: Kfb, k to end. 9 sts
Row 2: Pfb, p to end. 10 sts
Rows 3–4: Rep last 2 rows. 12 sts
Rows 5–16: Work in st st for 10 rows.
Row 17: *K1, kfb, k2; rep from * to end. 20 sts
Rows 18–42: St st 25 rows.
Row 43: *K1, k2tog, k1; rep. From * to end. 15 sts
Row 44: Purl.
Row 45: *K2tog, k1; rep from * to end. 10 sts
Break off yarn and draw yarn end through rem sts, pull tight and fasten off. Sew along the top of the hand. Leave the cast-on edge open and stuff.

BODY

(Make 1, starting at neck.)
With Funghi, cast on 16 sts.
Rows 1–2: Work in st st for 2 rows.
Row 3: K1, [kfb] 14 times, k1. 30 sts
Rows 4–8: Work in st st for 5 rows.
Row 9: K1, [kfb] 28 times, k1. 58 sts
Rows 10–36: Work in st st for 27 rows.
Row 37: K1, [k2tog] 28 times, k1. 30 sts
Rows 38–42: Work in st st for 5 rows.

Row 43: K1, [k2tog] 14 times, k1. 16 sts
Break off yarn and draw yarn end through rem sts, pull tight
and fasten. Sew along the side edge using mattress st and
stuff when three-quarters stitched. Continue to the cast-on
edge, then draw the yarn through the cast-on edge and pull
tight. Fasten and secure any loose threads.

HEAD

With Funghi, cast on 15 sts.
Rows 1–2: St st 2 rows.
Row 3: K1, [kfb] 13 times, k1. 28 sts
Row 5: K1, [kfb, k1] 13 times, k1. 41 sts
Row 4 and all even rows: Purl.
Rows 6–8: Work in st st for 3 rows.
Row 9: K1, [k1, kfb, k1] 13 times, k1. 54 sts
Rows 10–14: Work in st st for 5 rows.
Row 15: K1, [k1, kfb, k2] 13 times, k1. 67 sts
Rows 16–30: Work in st st for 15 rows.
Row 31: K10 [k2tog] 6 times, k21, [k2tog] 7 times, k10.
54 sts
Rows 32–36: St st 5 rows.
Row 37: K7, [k2tog] 6 times, k14, [k2tog] 7 times, k7.
Break off yarn. 41 sts
Rows 38–44: Add in Birch and st st 7 rows.
Row 45: K3, [k2tog] 6 times, k8, [k2tog] 7 times, k4. 28 sts
Row 47: *K2tog; rep from * to end. 14 sts
Row 48: *P2tog; rep from * to end. 7 sts
Cast off. Fold both ends of the cast-off edge to the middle
and sew together. Use mattress stitch to sew up the
remaining part of the head all the way to the cast-on edge.
Stuff and leave the gap open to add facial features.

NOSE

Cast on 24 sts in black.
Rows 1–2: St st 2 rows.
Row 3: K2tog, k8, [k2tog] twice, k8, k2tog. 20 sts
Row 4: P2tog, p6, [p2tog] twice, p6, p2tog. 16 sts
Row 5: [K2tog] 8 times.
Break off yarn and thread yarn end through the rem sts.
Fold both ends of the cast-off edge toward the middle

and sew up. Using mattress stitch, sew the side edge and stuff. Place in the centre of the snout and attach. Using the remaining yarn, sew a vertical line of back stitch downward and then create a semi-circle for the smile.

EARS

(Make 2.)
Cast on 22 sts in Funghi.
Row 1: K12, change to Birch, k10.
Row 2: P10 in Birch, P12 in Funghi.
Row 3–6: Repeat row 1–2.
Row 7: Using Funghi:, k2tog, k8, k2tog, change to Birch and k2tog, k6, k2tog. 18 sts
Row 8: P8 in Birch, k10 in Funghi.
Row 9: Using Funghi: k2tog, k6, k2tog, change to Birch and k2tog, k4, k2tog. 14 sts
Cast off.
Sew the top and side edge and attach to each side of the head.

EYES

(Make 2.)
With Birch, cast on 5 sts.
Rows 1 and 3: Knit.
Row 2 and 4: Purl.
Row 5: K2tog, k1, k2tog. 3 sts
Cast off.
For the pupil, chain 6 sts and join in a round. Attach to the centre of the eye, then fasten the eyes on each side of the head.

OUTFIT

TROUSERS

Starting from the bottom of the leg, cast on 24 sts in Fennel.
Rows 1–4: Work 4 rows in k1, p1 rib.
Row 5: Change to Pacific and [Kfb, k1] 12 times. 36 sts
Rows 6–8: St st 3 rows.
Row 9: [K1, kfb, k1] 12 times. 48 sts
Rows 10–28: St st 19 rows.
Break off yarn and place the remaining sts on a holding needle.
Knit another trouser leg.
Row 29: K48 sts and pick up and k the 48 sts from the holding needle. 96 sts
Rows 30–44: St st 15 rows.
Row 45: K1, [k1, k2tog, k2] 19 times. 77 sts
Row 47: K1, [k1, k2tog, k1] 19 times. 58 sts
Rows 48–51: Change to Fennel and work 4 rows in k1, p1 rib.
Cast off. Sew along the back of the trousers and up each leg.

JUMPER

Starting from the bottom of the jumper, cast on 30 sts in Fennel.
Rows 1–4: Work 4 rows in k1, p1 rib.
Rows 5–24: Change to Pacific and st st 20 rows.
Rows 25–28: Cast off 3 sts at the beginning of the next 4 rows. 18 sts
Rows 29–30: St st 2 rows.
Row 31: K4, cast off 10 sts, k4. 8 sts
Working on the first 4 sts: St st 3 rows, then cast off.
Repeat for the other 4 sts.
Make another piece, then sew the side and top edges together, leaving the arms and neck open.

SLEEVES

(Make 2.)

Cast on 24 sts in Fennel.

Rows 1–4: Work 4 rows in k1, p1 rib.

Rows 5–24: Change to Pacific and st 20 rows.

Rows 25–30: Cast off 3 sts at the beginning of each of the next 6 rows. 6 sts

Cast off.

Sew the sleeve seams and attach to the jumper.

POCKET

Cast on 16 sts in Fennel.

Rows 1–4: St st 4 rows.

Row 5: [K2tog] twice, k8, [k2tog] twice. 12 sts

Row 7: K2tog, k8, k2tog. 10 sts

Row 8: Purl.

Cast off.

Sew the cast-off and cast-on edge to the centre of the jumper.

HOOD

Cast on 72 sts in Fennel.

Rows 1–4: Work 4 rows in k1, p1 rib.

Rows 5–24: Change to Pacific and st st 20 rows.

Row 25: [K2, k2tog, k2] 12 times. 60 sts

Rows 26–28: St st 3 rows.

Row 29: [K2, k2tog, k1] 12 times. 48 sts

Rows 30–32: St st 3 rows.

Row 33: [K1, k2tog, k1] 12 times. 36 sts

Row 35: [K1, k2tog] 12 times. 24 sts

Cast off.

Fold the hood in half and sew along the cast-off edge. Attach the side edges to the collar of the jumper.

HEADBAND

Cast on 60 sts in Fennel.

Rows 1–2: Work 2 rows in k2, p2 rib.

Rows 3–6: Change to Pacific and st st 4 rows.

Rows 7–8: Change to Fennel and work 2 rows in k2, p2 rib.

Cast off.

Sew both side edges together.

TRAINERS

Starting from the sole of the shoe, cast on 25 sts in Cloud Dancer.

Row 1: Knit.

Row 2: K1, [kfb] 23 times, k1. 48 sts

Rows 3–8: Work in garter st for 6 rows.

Rows 9–18: Change to Fennel and st st 10 rows starting with a k row.

Row 19: K12, [k2tog] 4 times, yo, k2tog (18 sts) and leave the remaining 26 sts on a needle.

Rows 20 and 22: Purl.

Row 21: K10, [k2tog] 4 times. 14 sts

Row 23: K4, [k2tog] 4 times, yo, k2tog. 10 sts

Rows 24–26: St st 3 rows.

Cast off.

Pick up the next 4 sts and work as follows:

Rows 19–20: St st 2 rows.

Row 21: [Kfb] 4 times. 8 sts

Rows 22–26: St st 5 rows.

Cast off.

Pick up the remaining 22 sts and work as follows:

Row 19: K2tog, yo, [k2tog] 4 times, k to end. 18 sts

Row 20: P.

Row 21: [K2tog] 4 times, k to end. 14 sts

Row 22: P.

Row 23: K2tog, yo, [k2tog] 4 times, k to end. 10 sts

Rows 24–26: St st 3 rows.

Cast off.

Sew along the sole of the shoe and side edge. Make a twisted cord by cutting a 50 cm (18 in) length of Birch yarn. Fold the yarn strand in half and loop the centre point over a hook. Stretch the yarn and twist it consistently in the same direction. Unhook the twisted yarn and fold the cord in half while holding on to both ends. The yarn will twist itself into a tight cord. Knot each end and use this as a shoe lace. Make 2.

Master Wilfred Wabbit

Every child loves Christmas. This year why not add to the seasonal magic by making Santa a little helper? Master Wilfred Wabbit decided Easter was not quite his thing and teamed up with Team North Pole to help send presents to every child on Christmas Eve. He can often be seen dressed up as his idol.

You will need

2 x 50 g (2 oz) balls Wendy Merino DK, Silver (DK, 100 per cent merino wool, 116 m per ball)

2 x 50 g (2 oz) balls Wendy Merino DK, Birch (DK, 100 per cent merino wool, 116 m per ball)

2 x 50 g (2 oz) balls Wendy Merino DK, Persian Red (DK, 100 per cent merino wool, 116 m per ball)

2 x 50 g (2 oz) balls Wendy Merino DK, Jet (DK, 100 per cent merino wool, 116 m per ball)

Small amount of Maize yarn

3.5 mm (US 4) knitting needles

Wool needle

Toy stuffing

Holding needle

Crochet hook (optional)

LEGS
(Make 2, worked from sole of foot.)
With Silver, cast on 22 sts.
Row 1 and all odd rows: Purl.
Row 2: K1, [kfb] 20 times, k1. 42 sts
Rows 3–17: Work in st st for 15 rows.
Row 18: K7, [k2tog] 14 times, k7. 28 sts
Row 20: K7, [k2tog] 7 times, k7. 21 sts
Rows 21–49: Work in st st for 29 rows.
Row 50: K4, [k2tog] twice, k5, [k2tog] twice, k4. 17 sts
Cast off loosely. Sew up the sole of the foot first and continue along the back leg, leaving the cast-off edge open. Stuff firmly.

ARMS
(Make 2, work from top of arm.)
With Silver, cast on 8 sts.
Row 1: Kfb, k to end. 9 sts
Row 2: Pfb, p to end. 10 sts
Rows 3–4: Rep last 2 rows. 12 sts
Rows 5–6: Cast on 2 sts, work to end. 16 sts
Rows 7–16: Work in st st for 10 rows.
Row 17: *K1, kfb, k2; rep from * to end. 20 sts
Rows 18–42: St st 25 rows.
Row 43: *K1, k2tog, k1; rep. From * to end. 15 sts
Row 44: Purl.
Row 45: *K2tog, k1; rep from * to end. 10 sts
Break off yarn and draw yarn end through rem sts, pull tight and fasten off. Sew along the top of the hand. Leave the cast-on edge open and stuff.

BODY
(Make 1.)
With Silver, cast on 16 sts.
Rows 1–2: Work in st st for 2 rows.
Row 3: K1, [kfb] 14 times, k1. 30 sts
Rows 4–8: Work in st st for 5 rows.
Row 9: K1, [kfb] 28 times, k1. 58 sts
Rows 10–36: Work in st st for 27 rows.
Row 37: K1, [k2tog] 28 times, k1. 30 sts

Rows 38–42: Work in st st for 5 rows.
Row 43: K1, [k2tog] 14 times, k1. 16 sts
Break yarn and draw tail through rem sts, pull tight and fasten. Sew up along the side edge using mattress st and stuff when three-quarters stitched. Continue to the cast-on edge, then draw the yarn through the cast-on edge and pull tight. Fasten and secure any loose threads.

HEAD
With Silver, cast on 15 sts.
Rows 1–2: St st 2 rows.
Row 3: K1, [kfb] 13 times, k1. 28 sts
Row 4 and all even rows: Purl.
Row 5: K1, [kfb, k1] 13 times, k1. 41 sts
Rows 6–8: Work in st st.
Row 9: K1, [k1, kfb, k1] 13 times, k1. 54 sts
Rows 10–14: Work in st st for 5 rows.
Row 15: K1, [k1, kfb, k2] 13 times, k1. 67 sts
Rows 16–30: Work in st st for 15 rows.
Row 31: K12 [k2tog] 5 times, k23, [k2tog] 5 times, k12. 57 sts

Rows 32–36: St st 5 rows.
Row 37: K9, [k2tog] 5 times, k19, [k2tog] 5 times, k9. 47 sts
Row 38–40: St st 3 rows.
Row 41: K7, [k2tog] 5 times, k13, [k2tog] 5 times, k7. 37 sts
Row 43: K4, [k2tog] 5 times, k9, [k2tog] 5 times, k4. 27 sts
Row 45: K1, [k2tog] 5 times, k5, [k2tog] 5 times, k1. 17 sts
Row 46: P1, [p2tog] 8 times. 9 sts
Break off yarn and draw yarn end through rem sts, pull tight and fasten off. Fold both ends of the cast-off edge to the middle and sew together. Use mattress stitch to sew up the remaining part of the head all the way to the cast-on edge. Stuff and leave the gap open to add facial features.

EARS
(Make 2.)
Cast on 22 sts in Silver.
Rows 1–4: Work in st st.
Row 5: [K1, kfb, k7, kfb, k1] twice. 26 sts
Rows 6–8: Work in st st.

Row 9: [K1, kfb, k9, kfb, k1] twice. 30 sts

Rows 10–26: St st 17 rows.

Row 27: [K1, kfb, k11, kfb, k1] twice. 34 sts

Rows 28–40: St st 13 rows.

Row 41: [K1, kfb, k13, kfb, k1] twice. 38 sts

Rows 42–44: St st 3 rows beginning with a purl row.

Row 45: [K1, k2tog, k13, k2tog, k1] twice. 34 sts

Row 46 and all even rows: Purl.

Row 47: [K1, k2tog, k11, k2tog, k1] twice. 30 sts

Row 49: [K1, k2tog, k9, k2tog, k1] twice. 26 sts

Row 51: [K1, k2tog, k7, k2tog, k1] twice. 22 sts

Row 53: [K1, k2tog, k5, k2tog, k1] twice. 18 sts

Row 54: Purl.

Cast off and sew along the side edge. Attach to the side of the head. Attach to the front of the snout using the remaining yarn and sew a vertical line of back stitch downwards and then create a semi-circle for the smile.

EYES

(Make 2.)

With Birch, cast on 5 sts.

Rows 1 and 3: Knit.

Rows 2 and 4: Purl.

Row 5: K2tog, k1, k2tog. 3 sts

Cast off. Embroider a pupil using black yarn or chain 6 sts and join in a round. Attach to the centre of the eye, then fasten the eyes on each side of the head.

NOSE

Cast on 6 sts in Jet.

Rows 1–2: St st beginning with a knit row.

Row 3: Kfb, k4, kfb. 8 sts

Row 4: Purl.

Row 5: K2tog, k4, k2tog. 6 sts

Row 6: Purl.

Cast off.

OUTFIT

TROUSERS

Starting from the bottom of the leg, cast on 24 sts in Birch.

Rows 1–4: Garter st 4 rows (knit every row).

Row 5: Change to Persian Red and [Kfb, k1] 12 times. 36 sts

Rows 6–8: St st 3 rows.

Row 9: [K1, kfb, k1] 12 times. 48 sts

Rows 10–28: St st 19 rows.

Break off yarn and place the remaining sts on a holding needle. Knit another trouser leg.

Row 29: K48 sts and pick up and k the 48 sts waiting on the holding needle. 96 sts

Row 30–44: St st 15 rows.

Row 45: K1, [k1, k2tog, k2] 19 times. 77 sts

Row 46: Purl.

Row 47: K1, [k1, k2tog, k1] 19 times. 58 sts.

Cast off. Sew along the back of the trousers and up each leg.

HAT

Cast on 60 sts in Birch.

Rows 1–6: Garter st 6 rows. (Knit all rows)

Rows 7–22: Change to Persian Red and st st 16 rows, starting with a k row.

Row 23: [k5, k2tog, k5] 5 times. 55 sts

Rows 24–36: St st 13 rows.

Row 37: [k4, k2tog, k5] 5 times. 50 sts

Rows 38–48: St st 11 rows.

Row 49: [K4, k2tog, k4] 5 times. 45 sts

Rows 50–58: St st 9 rows.

Row 59: [K3, k2tog, k4] 5 times. 40 sts

Rows 60–66: St st 7 rows.

Row 67: [K3, k2tog, k3] 5 times. 35 sts

Rows 68–72: St st 5 rows.

Row 73: [K2, k2tog, k3] 5 times. 30 sts

Rows 74–76: St st 3 rows.

Row 77: [K2, k2tog, k2] 5 times. 25 sts

Rows 78–80: St st 3 rows.

Row 81: [K1, k2tog, k2] 5 times. 20 sts

Rows 82–84: St st 3 rows.

Rows 82–84: St st 3 rows.
Row 85: [K1, k2tog, k1] 5 times. 15 sts
Rows 86–88: St st 3 rows.
Row 89: [K2tog, k1] 5 times. 10 sts
Rows 90–92: St st 3 rows.
Row 93: [K2tog] 5 times. 5 sts
Break yarn and thread through remaining sts. Fasten off and sew along the side edge.

Using Birch, make a pompom for the hat by cutting two identical cardboard circles approximately 5.5 cm (2 in) in diameter with a small round hole 4 cm (1¾ in) diameter in the middle of each circle. Place the circles on top of each other and start to wind yarn round the circles and through the middle, ensuring no gaps are visible. Continue to wind the yarn until the circles are completely covered. Using the tip of a pair of scissors to cut between both circles along the outer edge. Draw a long piece of thread between the circles and fasten tightly with a knot in the centre. Cut through the remaining cardboard to free your pompom and trim to shape. Attach to the hat.

JUMPER
Starting from the rib of the jumper cast on 74 sts in Birch.
Rows 1–6: Garter st 6 rows. (Knit every row)
Rows 7–8: Change to Persian Red and st st, starting with a knit row.
Rows 9–12: Change to Jet and garter st 4 rows, knitwise.
Rows 13–16: Change to Persian Red and st st 3 rows.
Row 17: K1, [k5, k2tog, k5] 6 times, k1. 68 sts
Rows 18–20: St st 3 rows.
Row 21: K1, [k4, k2tog, k5] 6 times, k1. 62 sts
Rows 22–25: St st 4 rows.
Put the right-sided 16 and 30 sts on a needle holder and work on the left 16 sts as follows:
Row 26: Purl.
Row 27: [k2tog] twice, k12. 14 sts
Row 28 and all even rows: Purl.
Row 29: [k2tog] twice, k10. 12 sts
Rows 30–33: Work in st st.
Row 34: Cast off 6 sts, k6. 6 sts

Rows 35–36: St st 2 rows.

Cast off.

Join yarn to the middle 30 sts purlwise and work as follows:

Row 26: [P2tog] twice, p to end. 28 sts

Row 27: [k2tog] twice, k to end. 26 sts

Rows 28–29: Repeat rows 46–47. 22 sts

Row 30–33: Work in st st.

Row 34: P6, cast off 10, p6.

Rows 35–36: St st 2 rows.

Cast off.

Repeat rows 35–36 for the 6 sts on the other side.

Join yarn to the last 16 sts waiting and work as follows:

Row 26: [P2tog] twice, p to end. 14 sts

Row 27: Knit.

Rows 28–29: Repeat rows 26–27. 12 sts

Rows 30–32: Work in st st.

Row 33: Cast off 6 sts, k6. 6 sts.

Row 34–36: St st 3 rows.

Cast off.

SLEEVES

(Make 2, starting from the bottom of the sleeve.)

Cast on 28 sts in Birch.

Rows 1–4: Garter st 4 rows (knit all).

Rows 5–24: Change to Persian Red and work in st st.

Rows 25–30: Cast off 4 sts at the beginning of the next 6 rows. 4 sts

Cast off.

Sew the sides of the sleeves and attach to the jumper. Embroider a buckle using a small amount of yellow.

BOOTS

(Make 2.)

With Jet, cast on 32 sts.

Rows 1–14: Work in st st.

Row 15: Put first 11 sts on a holding needle and knit middle 10 sts only. Continue as follows on middle 10 sts:

Rows 15–24: Work in st st for 10 rows, then break yarn. 10 sts

Row 25: With RS facing, k11 held sts, pick up and knit 6 sts along the right side of the middle 10 st st rows, k10, pick up and k6 sts on the left side of the middle 10 st st rows, k11 held sts. 44 sts

Rows 26–32: Work in st st for 7 rows.

Leave 17 sts to the left and right on needle holder and knit along the middle 10 sts in Silver as follows:

Row 33: K9, k2tog (this is last st from middle and first st from held sts on side). Turn and repeat until a total 20 sts are left.

Cast off. Sew along the sole of the boot and along the side edge.

Master William Woof

A knitted puppy is for life and is sure to be loved by his new owner. Master William Woof is rather laid back and enjoys lounging around in a nice warm cosy place with a cup of hot cocoa.

You will need

1 x 50 g (2 oz) ball Wendy Merino DK, Spice (DK, 100 per cent merino wool, 116 m per ball)

1 x 50 g (2 oz) ball Wendy Merino DK, Crepe (DK, 100 per cent merino wool, 116 m per ball)

25 g (1 oz) Wendy Merino DK, Wind Chime (DK, 100 per cent merino wool, 116 m per ball)

25g (1 oz) Wendy Merino DK, Periwinkle (DK, 100 per cent merino wool, 116 m per ball)

25g (1 oz) Wendy Merino DK, Pacific (DK, 100 per cent merino wool, 116 m per ball)

Small amount of Jet and Birch for the facial features

3.5 mm (US 4) knitting needles

4 small buttons

Wool needle

Toy stuffing

Crochet hook

LEGS

(Make 2, worked from sole up.)

With Crepe, cast on 22 sts.

Row 1 and all odd rows: Purl.

Row 2: K1, [kfb] 20 times, k1. 42 sts

Rows 3–17: Work in st st for 15 rows.

Row 18: K7, [k2tog] 14 times, k7. 28 sts

Row 20: K7, [k2tog] 7 times, k7. 21 sts

Rows 21–49: Change to Spice and work in st st for 29 rows.

Row 50: K4, [k2tog] twice, k5, [k2tog] twice, k4. 17 sts

Cast off loosely. Sew up the bottom of the foot first and continue along the back edge, leaving the cast-off edge open. Stuff firmly.

ARMS

(Make 2.)

Starting from the top of the arms cast on 8 sts in Spice.

Row 1: Kfb, k to the end. 9 sts

Row 2: Pfb, p to the end. 10 sts

Rows 3–4: Repeat rows 1 and 2. 12 sts

Rows 5–6: Cast on 2 sts at the beginning of the next 2 rows. 16 sts

Rows 7–26: St st 20 rows.

Row 27: Change to Crepe and k1, [kfb, k1] 7 times, k1. 23 sts.

Row 28: Purl.

Row 29: K1, [k1, kfb, k1] 7 times, k1. 30 sts

Rows 30–34: St st 5 rows.

Finger 1

Row 35: Cast off 3 sts, k10 and turn. Continue to work on these 10 sts, leaving the other 15 sts waiting.

Rows 36–38: St st 3 rows.

Row 39: *K2tog; rep from * to end. 5 sts

Break yarn, thread yarn end through rem sts and fasten off.

Finger 2

Row 35: Cast on 3 sts, pick up the next 4 sts from needle and turn.

Row 36: Cast on 3 sts and work to end.

Rows 37–38: St st 2 rows.
Row 39: *K2tog; rep from * to end.

Finger 3
Pick up the next 10 sts on needle and repeat Finger 1.
Join yarn to the last 3 sts and cast off.
Sew along the inside of all 3 fingers, then join the base of
the second finger to the cast-off edge. Sew along the side
of the arm, stuff and attach to the body.

BODY
Starting at neck, cast on 16 sts using Spice.
Rows 1–2: Work in st st for 2 rows.
Row 3: K1, [kfb] 14 times, k1. 30 sts
Rows 4–8: Work in st st for 5 rows.
Row 9: K1, [kfb] 28 times, k1. 58 sts
Rows 10–36: Work in st st for 27 rows.
Row 37: K1, [k2tog] 28 times, k1. 30 sts
Rows 38–42: Work in st st for 5 rows.
Row 43: K1, [k2tog] 14 times, k1. 16 sts
Break yarn and draw yarn end through rem sts, pull tight
and fasten. Sew up along the side edge using mattress st
and stuff when three-quarters full. Continue to the cast-on
edge, then draw the yarn through the cast-on edge and pull
tight. Fasten and secure any loose threads.

HEAD
With Spice, cast on 15 sts.
Rows 1–2: St st 2 rows.
Row 3: K1, [kfb] 13 times, k1. 28 sts
Row 4 and all even rows: Purl.
Row 5: K1, [kfb, k1] 13 times, k1. 41 sts
Rows 6–8: Work in st st for 3 rows.
Row 9: K1, [k1, kfb, k1] 13 times, k1. 54 sts
Rows 10–14: Work in st st for 5 rows.
Row 15: K1, [k1, kfb, k2] 13 times, k1. 67 sts
Rows 16–30: Work in st st for 15 rows.
Row 31: K10 [k2tog] 6 times, k21, [k2tog] 7 times, k10.
54 sts
Rows 32–36: St st 5 rows.

Row 37: K5, [k2tog] 9 times, k8, [k2tog] 9 times, k5. 36 sts

Row 38: Change to Crepe and purl.

Row 39: K5, [k1, kfb] 5 times, k8, [k1, kfb] 4 times, k5. 45 sts

Rows 40–42: St st 3 rows.

Row 43: K5, [k1, kfb, k1] 5 times, k8, [k1, kfb, k1] 4 times, k5. 54 sts

Row 45: K5, [k1, k2tog, k1] 5 times, k8, [k1, k2tog, k1] 4 times, k5. 45 sts

Row 47: K5, [k1, k2tog] 5 times, k8, [k1, k2tog] 4 times, k5. 36 sts

Row 49: K5, [k2tog] 5 times, k8, [k2tog] 4 times, k5. 27 sts

Row 51: K1, [k2tog] 13 times. 14 sts

Cast off.

Fold both ends of the cast-off edge to the middle and sew together. Use mattress stitch to sew up the remaining part of the head all the way to the cast-on edge. Stuff and leave the gap open to add facial features.

EARS

(Make 2)

Cast on 12 sts in Crepe.

Row 1: K1, [kfb] 10 times, k1. 22 sts

Rows 2–4: St st 3 rows, using p for even rows and k for odd rows.

Row 5: [K1, kfb, k7, kfb, k1] twice. 26 sts

Rows 6–8: St st 3 rows as before.

Row 9: [K1, kfb, k9, kfb, k1] twice. 30 sts

Rows 10–36: St st 27 rows.

Row 37: [K1, k2tog, k9, k2tog, k1] twice. 26 sts

Row 38: Purl.

Row 39: [K1, k2tog, k7, k2tog, k1] twice. 22 sts

Row 40: Purl.

Row 41: [K1, k2tog, k5, k2tog, k1] twice. 18 sts

Row 42: Purl.

Cast off and sew along the side edge. Attach to the side of the head

EYE PATCH

Cast on 32 sts in Crepe.

Row 1 and 3: Purl.

Row 2: [K1, k2tog, k1] 8 times. 24 sts

Row 4: [K1, k2tog] 8 times. 16 sts

Row 5: [P2tog] 8 times. 8 sts

Row 6: [K2tog] 4 times. 4 sts

Break yarn and thread yarn end through rem. sts. Join in a round and attach to the head, just above the colour change.

NOSE

Cast on 24 sts in black.

Rows 1–2: St st 2 rows.

Row 3: K2tog, k8, [k2tog] twice, k8, k2tog. 20 sts

Row 4: P2tog, p6, [p2tog] twice, p6, p2tog. 16 sts

Row 5: [K2tog] 8 times. 8 sts

Break yarn and thread yarn end through the rem sts. Sew up along the side, stuff and attach to the front of the head. Using the remaining yarn and sew a lopsided semi-circle in back stitch for the smirk.

EYES

(Make 2)

With Birch, cast on 5 sts.

Rows 1 and 3: Knit.

Rows 2 and 4: Purl.

Row 5: K2tog, k1, k2tog. 3 sts

Cast off. Embroider a pupil using black yarn or chain 6 sts and join in a round. Attach to the centre of the eye, then fasten the eyes on each side of the head, positioning one eye to the bottom part of the patch and a second spaced evenly above the snout.

OUTFIT

BOOTS

(Make 2.)

With Wind Chime, cast on 24 sts.

Row 1 and all odd rows: Purl.

Row 2: K1, [kfb] 22 times, k1. 46 sts

Rows 3–17: Work in st st for 15 rows.

Row 18: K8, [k2tog] 15 times, k8. 31 sts

Cast off and sew along the heel and side.

BOOT CUFFS

With Wind Chime, cast on 15 sts.

Rows 1–50: Work in k1, p1 rib st for 50 rows, beg with a k row.

Row 51: K1, p1, k1, skpsso, yo, continue in rib stitch until the last 5 sts, yo, skpsso, k1, p1, k1. 15 sts

Rows 52–55: Continue in rib for 4 rows.

Cast off. Wrap around top of the boot and sew in place. Sew two buttons on the side, level with the eyelets.

TROUSERS

With Periwinkle, cast on 24 sts.

Row 1: [Kfb, k1] 12 times. 36 sts

Rows 2–4: St st 3 rows, beg with a purl row.

Row 5: [K1, kfb, k1] 12 times. 48 sts

Rows 6–18: St st 13 rows.

Break yarn and place rem sts on a holder. Knit another trouser leg. 96 sts

Row 19: K across sts then k across sts on holding needle.

Rows 20–40: St st 21 rows.

Row 41: K1, [k1, k2tog, k2] 19 times. 77 sts

Row 43: K1, [k1, k2tog, k1] 19 times. 58 sts

Cast off. Sew along the back of the trousers and sew up each leg.

JUMPER

Back panel

Starting from the rib, cast on 32 sts in Pacific.

Rows 1–4: Work 4 rows in k2, p2 rib, beg first row with k1 and ending row with p1. Keep remaining rib as set.

Rows 5–24: St st 20 rows, beg with a k row.

Rows 25–28: Cast off 3 sts at the beginning of the next 4 rows. 20 sts

Rows 29–30: St st 2 rows.

Row 31: K5, cast off 10 sts, k5. 10 sts

Rows 32–34: Working on the first 5 sts: St st 3 rows.

Cast off.

Repeat for the other 5 sts.

Front panel

Starting from the rib, cast on 32 sts in Pacific.

Rows 1–4: Work 4 rows in k2, p2 rib, beg first row with k1 and ending row with p1. Keep remaining rib as set.

Row 5–24: St st 20 rows beg with a purl row.

Row 25: Cast off 3 sts, k9 (leaving 10 sts on needle), cast off 6 sts, k to end. 13 sts

Row 26: Cast off 3 sts, p to end. 10 sts

Row 27: K2tog, k to end. 9 sts

Rows 28–29: Repeat row 26–27. 5 sts

Rows 30–34: St st 5 rows.

Cast off.

Rejoin yarn to the 10 sts on needle and work as follows:

Row 26: P2tog, p to end. 9 sts

Row 27: Cast off 3 sts, k to end. 6 sts

Row 28: As row 26. 5 sts

Rows 29–34: St st 6 rows.

Cast off. Sew the shoulder and side seams, leaving a gap to attach the arms.

SLEEVES

(Make 2.)

Cast on 24 sts in Pacific.

Rows 1–4: Work 4 rows in k2, p2 rib, beg first row with k1 and ending row with p1. Keep remaining rib as set.

Rows 5–24: St st 20 rows.

Rows 25–30: Cast off 3 sts at the beginning of next 6 rows. 6 sts

Cast off.

Sew the sides of the sleeves together then attach to the jumper.

Collar

Cast on 50 sts in Pacific.

Rows 1–8: Work 8 rows in k2, p2 rib.

Cast off and sew the side edge to the 6 cast-off sts on the front panel, then attach the cast-on edge to the rest of the neckline. Attach the other side edge to the front of the panel again.

HAT

Cast on 64 sts in Wind Chime.

Rows 1–8: Work 8 rows in k2, p2 rib, beg first row with k1 and ending row with p1. Keep remaining rib as set.

Rows 9–38: St st 30 rows, beg with a k row.

Row 39: K2, [k4, k2tog, k4] 6 times, k2. 58 sts

Row 40 and all even rows: Purl.

Row 41: K2, [k3, k2tog, k4] 6 times, k2. 52 sts

Row 43: K2, [k3, k2tog, k3] 6 times, k2. 46 sts

Row 45: K2, [k2, k2tog, k3] 6 times, k2. 40 sts

Row 47: K2, [k2, k2tog, k2] 6 times, k2. 34 sts

Row 49: K2, [k1, k2tog, k2] 6 times, k2. 28 sts

Row 51: K2, [k1, k2tog, k1] 6 times, k2. 22 sts

Row 53: K2, [k2tog, k1] 6 times, k2. 16 sts

Row 55: [K2tog] 8 times. 8 sts

Break off yarn and thread yarn end through remaining sts. Fasten tightly and sew along the side edge.

57

Miss Felicia Fox

Spring is most definitely my favourite time of year. It's not too cold and not too hot and apart from the occasional shower, it reminds me of new beginnings when the trees turn green and the flowers start to bloom. Miss Felicia Fox is an expert when it comes to gardening. She will brave the April showers in her trendy wellington boots to tend to her much-loved patch of green.

You will need

1 x 50 g (2 oz) ball Wendy Merino DK, Otter (DK, 100 per cent merino wool, 116 m per ball)

1 x 50 g (2 oz) ball Wendy Merino DK, Birch (DK, 100 per cent merino wool, 116 m per ball)

1 x 50 g (2 oz) ball Wendy Merino DK, Cadet (DK, 100 per cent merino wool, 116 m per ball)

1 x 50 g (2 oz) ball Wendy Merino DK, Watermelon (DK, 100 per cent merino wool, 116 m per ball)

A small amount of Jet yarn for features

2 small buttons

3.5 mm (US 4) knitting needles

Wool needle

Toy stuffing

Pins

Holding needle and crochet hook

LEG
(Make 2.)
Starting from the sole of the foot, cast on 22 sts in Otter, changing to Birch after 3 rows and continue to alternate in the same way.
Row 1 and all odd rows: Purl.
Row 2: K1, [kfb 1] 20 times, k1. 42 sts
Rows 3–17: St st 15 rows.
Row 18: K7, [k2tog] 14 times, k7. 28 sts
Row 20: K7, [k2tog] 7 times, k7. 21 sts
Row 21–49: St st 29 rows.
Row 50: K4, [k2tog] 2 times, k5, k2tog] 2 times, k4. 17 sts
Row 51: Cast off loosely.
Sew the legs, starting from the base of the foot, all the way to the top. Leave the top part open to allow stuffing. For best results use mattress stitch to sew up all the pieces.

ARMS
(Make 2.)
Starting from the top of the arms, cast on 8 sts in Otter.
Row 1: Kfb1, k to the end. 9 sts
Row 2: Pfb1, p to the end. 10 sts
Rows 3–4: Repeat the last 2 rows. 12 sts
Rows 5–6: Cast on 2 sts at the beginning of the next 2 rows. 16 sts
Rows 7–26: St st 20 rows.
Rows 27–28: Change to Birch and st st 2 rows.
Row 29: Cast off 3 sts, then work fingers as follows:

Finger 1
Row 29: [Kfb] 3 times, turn. 6 sts
Rows 30–32: St st 3 rows.
Row 33: [K2tog] 3 times. 3 sts
Break off yarn and thread yarn end through the remaining sts. Pull tight and fasten.

Finger 2

Join the yarn to the next 2 sts and knit as follows:

Row 29: Cast on 2 st, k to end. 4 sts

Row 30: Cast on 2 sts, p to end. 6 sts

Rows 31–32: St st 2 rows.

Row 33: [K2tog] 3 times. 3 sts

Break off yarn and thread through the remaining sts. Pull tight and fasten off.

Repeat finger 2 and finger 1, then cast off the remaining 3 sts.

Sew up the fingers one by one and then join the bottom of the two middle fingers to the 3 cast-off sts at the side of the hand. Sew the arms, leaving a gap at the top for stuffing and connecting to the body.

BODY

Starting from the neck, cast on 16 sts in Otter.

Rows 1–2: St st 2 rows.

Row 3: K1, [kfb 1] 14 times, k1. 30 sts

Rows 4–8: St st 5 rows.

Row 9: K1, [kfb 1] 28 times, k1. 58 sts

Rows 10–36: St st 27 rows.

Row 37: K1, [k2tog] 28 times, k1. 30 sts

Row 38–42: St st 5 rows.

Row 43: K1, [k2tog] 14 times, k1. 16 sts

Break yarn and thread yarn end through the remaining sts. Pull tight and fasten off. Sew up along the side edge using mattress st and stuff when three-quarters stitched. Continue to the cast-on edge, then draw the yarn through the cast-on edge and pull tight. Fasten and secure any loose threads.

HEAD

Cast on 20 sts using Otter.

Row 1: *K1, [kfb] 3 times, k1; rep from * to end. 32 sts

Row 2 all other even rows: Purl.

Row 3: *K1, [kfb] twice, k1; rep from * to end. 48 sts

Row 5: *K6, [kfb] 4 times, k4, [kfb] 4 times, k6; rep from * to end. 64 sts

Rows 6–8: St st 3 rows.

Row 9: *K8, [kfb] 4 times, k8, [kfb] 4 times, k8; rep from * to end. 80 sts

Rows 10–14: St st 5 rows.

Row 15: *K12, [kfb] 4 times, k8, [kfb] 4 times, k12; rep from * to end. 96 sts

Row 17: *K12, [k2tog] 4 times, k8, [k2tog] 4 times, k12; rep from * to end. 80 sts

Rows 18–20: St st 3 rows.

Row 21: *K8, [k2tog] 4 times, k8, [k2tog] 4 times, k8; rep from * to end. 64 sts

Row 23: *K6, [k2tog] 4 times, k4, [k2tog] 4 times, k6; rep from * to end. 48 sts

Row 25: *K1, [k2tog] twice, k1; rep from * to end. 32 sts

Row 27: *K1, [k2tog] 3 times, k1; rep from * to end. 20 sts

Row 28: *P2tog; rep from * to end. 10 sts.

Break off yarn and thread yarn end through the remaining stitches. Pull tight and fasten off. For the head, sew along the side and leave the bottom part open for stuffing and adding facial features.

Attach the head, arms and legs to the body.

EARS

(Make 2.)

Cast on 24 sts in Otter.

Rows 1–2: St st 2 rows.

Row 3: *K1, k2tog, k6, k2tog, k1; rep from * to end. 20 sts

Row 4 and all even rows: Purl.

Row 5: *K1, k2tog, k4, k2tog, k1; rep from * to end. 16 sts

Row 7: *K1, k2tog, k2, k2tog, k1; rep from * to end. 12 sts

Row 9: *K1, [k2tog] twice, k1; rep from * to end. 8 sts

Row 11: *K1, k2tog, k1; rep from * to end. 6 sts

Row 12: [P2tog] 3 times. 3 sts

Cast off.

Fold the ears in half and sew along the seam. Attach to the head at the cast-on edge.

SNOUT

Cast on 32 sts in Birch.

Rows 1–4: St st 4 rows (purl all even rows)

Row 5: *K1, k2tog, k1; rep from * to end. 24 sts

Row 6 and all even rows: Purl.

Row 7: *K1, k2tog; rep from * to end. 16 sts

Row 9: *K2tog; rep from * to end. 8 sts

Cast off and set aside.

NOSE

Cast on 12 sts in Otter.

Rows 1–2: St st 2 rows.

Row 3: K2tog, k8, k2tog. 10 sts

Row 4 and all even rows: Purl.

Row 5: K2tog, k6, k2tog. 8 sts

Row 7: Change to Jet. K2tog, k4, k2tog. 6 sts

Row 9: K2tog, k2, k2tog. 4 sts

Row 11: [K2tog] twice. 2 sts

Cast off.

Join each side of the nose to the side and cast-off edges of the snout to create a full circle. Sew in place on the head and stuff before completing the sewing. Using back stitch sew a vertical line downwards and then create a semi-circle for the smile.

EYES

(Make 2.)

Cast on 5 sts in Birch.

Rows 1–4: St st 4 rows.

Row 5: K2tog, k1, k2tog. 3 sts

Cast off.

Embroider a pupil on each eye or chain 6 sts and join in a round. Attach to the centre of the eye, then fasten the eyes on each side of the head. For the eyelashes, unravel some black yarn and stitch three curved lines of back stitches above each eye. Pin the eyes in place and sew on the head.

OUTFIT

DUNGAREES

Starting from the leg, cast on 24 sts in Cadet.

Row 1: [kfb, k1] 12 times. 36 sts

Rows 2–4: St st 3 rows.

Row 5: [K1, kfb, k1] 12 times. 48 sts

Rows 6–8: St st 3 rows.

Break yarn and place the rem sts on a holding needle. Knit a second trouser leg.

Row 9: K48 sts, pick up and k the 48 sts on holding needle. 96 sts

Rows 10–30: St st 21 rows.

Row 31: K1, [k1, k2tog, k2] 19 times. 77 sts

Row 32 and ever even row: Purl.

Row 33: K1, [k1, k2tog, k1] 19 times. 58 sts

Row 34: Cast off 19 sts, p to end. 39 sts

Row 35: Cast off 19 sts, k to end. 20 sts

Rows 36–44: St st 9 rows.

Cast off. Sew along the back of the trousers and sew up each leg.

Straps

(Make 2.)

Using Cadet, cast on 34 sts.

Row 1: Purl.

Row 2: K2tog, yo, k to end.

Row 3: Purl.

Cast off. Attach the side edge (without the yo hole) to the back of the trousers and cross over at back of body. Attach 2 small buttons to the front of the dungarees and stitch in place.

BOOTS

(Make 2.)

With Cadet, cast on 32 sts.

Rows 1–3: Knit.

Row 4: K5, cast off 6 sts, k10, cast off 6 sts, k5. 20 sts

Row 5: Change to Watermelon and k5, cast on 5 sts, k10, cast on 5 sts, k5. 30 sts

Rows 6–12: St st for 7 rows.

Rows 13–22: Put 10 sts on a holding needle and work on the middle 10 sts only as follows:

Knit, break yarn. 10 sts

Row 23: With RS facing, k10 held sts, pick up and k6 sts

along right side of last 10 st st rows, k10, pick up and k6 sts on the left side of last 10 st st rows, k10 sts left on needle. 42 sts

Rows 24–30: Work in st st for 7 rows.

Leave 16 sts to the left and right on spare needles and knit along the middle 10 sts in Cadet as follows:

Row 31: K9, k2tog (this is last st from middle and first st from held sts on side). Turn and repeat until a total 20 sts are left.

Cast off. Sew along the sole of the boot and along the side edge. Make a second boot.

TOP

Using Watermelon, cast on 60 sts.

Rows 1–16: St st.

Row 17: K13, cast off 4, k26, cast off 4, k13.

Leave the first 13 and 26 sts on a needle and work on the left 13 sts as follows:

Row 18 and all even rows: Purl.

Row 19: [K2tog] twice, k9. 11 sts

Row 20 and all even rows: Purl.

Row 21: [K2tog] twice, k7. 9 sts

Rows 22–25: St st 4 rows.

Row 26: Cast off 6 sts, p to end. 3 sts

Rows 27–28: St st 2 rows.

Cast off.

Re join yarn to the 26 sts on needle purlwise and work as follows:

Row 18: [P2tog] twice, p to end. 24 sts

Row 19: [k2tog] twice, k to end. 22 sts

Rows 20–21: Repeat row 56–57. 18 sts

Rows 22–25: St st 4 rows.

Row 26: P4, cast off 10, p4.

Rows 27–28: St st 2 rows.

Cast off.

Repeat rows 27–28 for the 4 sts on the other side.

Re join yarn to the last 13 sts on needle and work as follows:

Row 18: [P2tog] twice, p to end. 11 sts

Row 19: Knit.

Rows 20–21: Repeat row 56–57. 9 sts

Rows 22–24: St st 3 rows.

Row 25: Cast off 6 sts, k3. 3 sts.

Rows 26–28: St st 3 rows.

Cast off. Sew along the back edge and across the shoulder seams.

SLEEVES

Starting from the cuff, cast on 20 sts in Watermelon.

Rows 1–4: St st 4 rows.

Rows 5–10: Cast off 3 sts at the beginning of the next 6 rows and work to the end. 2 sts

Cast off and sew along the side edge. Attach to the armholes.

FLOWER

Cast on 16 sts using Watermelon.

Row 1: *K1, yo; rep from * to last st, k1. 31 sts

Row 2: Knit.

Row 3: [K1, yo, k2tog] 5 times, [k2, yo, k2tog] 4 times.

Row 4: Cast off 30 sts, k1. 1 st

Row 5: [Cast on 4 sts, pick up 1 st through eyelet] 3 times, [cast on 5 sts, pick up 1 st through eyelet] 3 times, [cast on 6 sts, pick up 1 st through eyelet] twice, cast on 7 sts, pick up 1 st through eyelet.

Cast off. 55 sts

Roll up the flower and add a few stitches at the base to gather.

BRACELET

Cast on 18 sts in Cadet.

Rows 1–4: Work in k2, p2 rib.

Cast off.

Sew along the edge and attach the flower to the top.

Miss Marcia Mouse

Miss Marcia Mouse adores dressing in her Sunday best and loves to attend a party. She likes to be the centre of attention wherever she goes and always dresses stylishly.

You will need

2 x 50 g (2 oz) balls Wendy Merino DK, Smoke (DK, 100 per cent merino wool, 116 m per ball)

1 x 50 g (2 oz) ball Wendy Merino DK, Mulberry (DK, 100 per cent merino wool, 116 m per ball)

1 x 50 g (2 oz) ball Wendy Merino DK, Crepe (DK, 100 per cent merino wool, 116 m per ball)

25 g (2 oz) Wendy Merino DK, Birch (DK, 100 per cent merino wool, 116 m per ball)

Small amount of Carnation for the nose and Jet (black) for the eyes

2 small buttons for the shoes

3.5 mm (US 4) knitting needles

Wool needle and crochet hook (optional)

Toy filling

Holding needle

SPECIAL INSTRUCTIONS

wyib sl1pw: With yarn in back slip 1 purlwise. **wyif sl1pw:** With yarn in front slip 1 purlwise

ssk: Slip the next 2 stitches, one at a time, knitwise to the right-hand needle. Purl them together through the back loops.

LEGS

(Make 2, working from bottom of foot.)
With Smoke, cast on 22 sts.
Row 1 and all odd rows: Purl.
Row 2: K1, [kfb] 20 times, k1. 42 sts
Rows 3–17: Work in st st for 15 rows.
Row 18: K7, [k2tog] 14 times, k7. 28 sts
Row 19: Purl.
Row 20: K7, [k2tog] 7 times, k7. 21 sts
Rows 21–49: Work in st st for 29 rows.
Row 50: K4, [k2tog] twice, k5, [k2tog] twice, k4. 17 sts
Cast off loosely. Sew up the bottom of the foot first and continue along the back edge, leaving the cast-off edge open. Stuff well.

ARMS

(Make 2, working from top of arm.)
With Smoke, cast on 8 sts.
Row 1: Kfb, knit to end. 9 sts
Row 2: Pfb, purl to end. 10 sts
Rows 3–4: Rep last 2 rows. 12 sts
Rows 5–6: Cast on 2 sts, work to end. 16 sts
Rows 7–28: Work in st st for 24 rows.
Rows 29–30: Cast on 6 sts at the beginning of the next 2 rows, work to the end. 28 sts
Rows 31–34: St st 4 rows.
Rows 35–36: Cast off 6 sts at the beginning of the next 2 rows, work to end. 16 sts
Rows 37–42: St st 6 rows.
Row 43: [K2tog, k4, k2tog] twice, 12 sts
Row 44: Purl.
Row 45: [K2tog, k2, k2tog] twice. 8 sts
Break yarn and draw yarn end through rem sts, pull tight and fasten off. Sew along the top of the hand and across the thumb and arm. Leave the cast-on edge open and stuff.

BODY

(Make 1 starting at neck.)
With Smoke, cast on 16 sts.
Rows 1–2: Work in st st for 2 rows.

Row 3: K1, [kfb] 14 times, k1. 30 sts
Rows 4–8: Work in st st for 5 rows.
Row 9: K1, [kfb] 28 times, k1. 58 sts
Rows 10–36: Work in st st for 27 rows.
Row 37: K1, [k2tog] 28 times, k1. 30 sts
Rows 38–42: Work in st st for 5 rows.
Row 43: K1, [k2tog] 14 times, k1. 16 sts
Break yarn and draw yarn end through rem sts, pull tight
and fasten. Sew up along the side edge using mattress st
and stuff when three-quarters stitched. Continue to the
cast-on edge, then draw the yarn through the cast-on edge
and pull tight. Fasten and secure any loose threads.

HEAD
With Smoke, cast on 15 sts.
Rows 1–2: St st 2 rows.
Row 3: K1, [kfb] 13 times, k1. 28 sts
Row 4 and all even rows: Purl.
Row 5: K1, [kfb, k1] 13 times, k1. 41 sts
Rows 6–8: Work in st st for 3 rows.

Row 9: K1, [k1, kfb, k1] 13 times, k1. 54 sts
Rows 10–14: Work in st st for 5 rows.
Row 15: K1, [k1, kfb, k2] 13 times, k1. 67 sts
Rows 16–30: Work in st st for 15 rows.
Row 31: K2 [k3, k2tog, k3] 8 times, k1. 59 sts
Rows 32–36: St st 5 rows.
Row 37: K2, [k2, k2tog, k3] 8 times, k1. 51 sts
Rows 38–42: St st 5 rows.
Row 43: K2, [k2, k2tog, k2] 8 times, k1. 43 sts
Rows 44–46: St st 3 rows.
Row 47: K2, [k1, k2tog, k2] 8 times, k1. 35 sts
Rows 48–50: St st 3 rows.
Row 51: K2, [k1, k2tog, k1] 8 times, k1. 27 sts
Row 53: K2, [k1, k2tog] 8 times, k1. 19 sts
Row 55: K2, [k2tog] 8 times, k1. 11 sts
Cast off and sew along the side. Leave a gap for stuffing and
easy access to add facial features.

EARS

(Make 2)

With Smoke, cast on 35 sts.

Row 1: [K1, kfb, k14, kfb] twice, k1. 39 sts

Rows 2–14: St st 13 rows.

Row 15: [K1, k2tog, k14, k2tog] twice, k1. 35 sts

Row 16 and all even rows: Purl.

Row 17: [K1, k2tog, k12, k2tog] twice, k1. 31 sts

Row 19: [K1, k2tog, k2tog, k6, k2tog, k2tog] twice, k1. 23 sts

Cast off. Fold the piece in half lengthwise and sew along the edge.

NOSE

With Carnation, cast on 10 sts.

Row 1: *Kfb; rep from * to end. 20 sts

Rows 2–4: St st 3 rows.

Row 5: *K2tog; rep from * to end. 10 sts

Row 6: *P2tog; rep from * to end. 5 sts

Break yarn and draw yarn end through rem sts, pull tight and fasten off. Sew along the side and stuff.

EYES

(Make 2)

With Crepe, cast on 5 sts.

Rows 1 and 3: Knit.

Rows 2 and 4: Purl.

Row 5: K2tog, k1, k2tog. 3 sts

Cast off.

For the pupil chain 6 sts and join in a round. Attach to the centre of the eye, then fasten the eyes on each side of the head.

For the eyelashes unravel some black yarn or use embroidering thread to add a three curved lines of back stitches above each eye.

OUTFIT

DRESS

With Mulberry, cast on 89 sts.

Rows 1 and 2: Knit.

Row 3: Change to Crepe and k1, *wyib sl1pw, k1, repeat from * to end.

Row 4: K1, *wyif sl1pw, k1, repeat from * to end.

Row 5: Change to Mulberry and knit.

Row 6: Knit.

Row 7: Change to Crepe and k2, * wyib sl1pw, k1, repeat from * to last st, k1.

Row 8: K2, * wyif sl1pw, k1, repeat from * to last st, k1.

Row 9: Change to Mulberry and knit.

Rows 10–49: Repeat rows 2–8 five times.

Row 50: K3, [k2, k2tog, k2] 14 times, k2. 75 sts

Row 51: [K2, k2tog, k1] 15 times. 60 sts

Row 52: Knit.

Row 53: Change to Crepe and K2, [k2, k2tog, k3] 8 times, k2. 52 sts

Rows 54–58: St st 5 rows.

Row 59: K11, cast off 4 sts, k22, cast off 4, k11. 44 sts

Left side of dress

Row 60: P. 11 sts

Row 61: K2tog, k to end. 10 sts

Rows 62–63: Repeat the last 2 rows. 9 sts

Row 64: Cast off 6 sts, p to end, cut yarn and leave the remaining 3 sts on a spare needle.

Middle part of the dress

Pick up the middle 22 sts on purl side and knit as follows:

Row 60: P2tog, p to end. 21 sts

Row 61: K2tog, k to end. 20 sts

Rows 62–63: Repeat the last 2 rows. 18 sts

Row 64: P3, cast off 12 sts, p3. Cut yarn and leave the 2 x 3 sts on holder.

Right side of dress

Pick up the last 11 sts on purl side and knit as follows:

Row 60: P2tog, p to end. 10 sts

Row 61: Knit.

Rows 62–63: Repeat the last 2 rows. 9 sts

Rows 64: P3, cast off 6 sts. 3 sts

Row 65: Join yarn to the right 3 sts and knit as follows to create the strap for the dress on the right side: K3, cast on 3 sts, k3 (these were left waiting), turn. 9 sts

Row 66: Purl.

Row 67: Cast off 9 sts and repeat these last 3 rows on the other 2 sets of 3 sts on the left side.

Using mattress st sew up along the side edge of the dress and join the shoulders together.

LEFT SHOE

With Crepe, cast on 24 sts.

Row 1 and all odd rows: Purl.

Row 2: K1, [kfb] 22 times, k1. 46 sts

Rows 3–17: Work in st st for 15 rows.

Row 18: K8, [k2tog] 15 times, k8. 31 sts

Row 19: P8, cast off 15 sts, p8.

Row 20: K8, cast on 18 sts and turn, leaving the other 8 sts on a holding needle. 26 sts

Row 21: Purl.

Row 22: K24, yo, k2tog. 26 sts

Row 23: Purl.

Cast off.

Join yarn to the 8 sts held and work as follows:

Rows 20–22: St st 3 rows.

Cast off and sew along the heel and side. Attach a button to the side of the shoe.

RIGHT SHOE

Work as left shoe until row 18. 8 sts

Rows 20–23: St st 4 rows.

Cast off.

Join yarn to the 8 sts on hold and work as follows:

Row 20: Cast on 18 sts, k to end. 26 sts

Row 21: P.

Row 22: K2tog, yo, k to end.
Row 23: Purl.
Cast off and make up as first shoe.

SHAWL

Using Birch, cast on 19 sts.
Rows 1–2: K both rows.
Row 3: K2, yo, k2, sl1, k2tog, psso, k2, yo, ssk, yo, sl1, k2tog, psso, yo, k3, yo, k2. 19 sts
Row 4 and all even rows: K2, p to last 2 sts, k2. 19 sts
Row 5: K2, yo, k2, sl1, k2tog, psso, k2, yo, sl1, k2tog, psso, yo, k5, yo, k2. 19 sts
Row 7: K2, yo, k1, yo, k1, sl1, k2tog, psso, k1, yo, ssk, yo, k2, sl1, k2tog, psso, k2, yo, k2. 19 sts
Row 9: K2, yo, k3, yo, sl1, k2tog, psso, yo, ssk, yo, k2, sl1, k2tog, psso, k2, yo, k2. 19 sts
Row 11: K2, yo, k5, yo, sl1, k2tog, psso, yo, k2, sl1, k2tog, psso, k2, yo, k2. 19 sts
Row 13: K2, yo, k2, sl1, k2tog, psso, k2, yo, ssk, yo, k1, sl1, k2tog, psso, k1, yo, k1, yo, k2. 19 sts
Rows 15–86: Repeat rows 2–14.
Rows 87–88: K2 rows.
Cast off and block.

PURSE

Using Crepe, cast on 20 sts.
Rows 1–2: St st 2 rows.
Row 3: [K2, yo, k2] 5 times. 25 sts
Row 4 and all even rows: Purl.
Row 5: [K2, kfb, k2] 5 times. 30 sts
Row 7: [K3, kfb, k2] 5 times. 35 sts
Row 9: [K3, kfb, k3] 5 times. 40 sts
Rows 10–14: St st 5 rows.
Row 15: [K2, k2tog, k1] 8 times. 32 sts
Row 17: [K1, k2tog, k1] 8 times. 24 sts
Row 19: [K1, k2tog] 8 times. 16 sts
Row 21: [K2tog] 8 times. 8 sts
Row 22: [P2tog] 4 times. 4 sts
Break yarn and thread yarn end through rem sts. Pull tight and fasten off. Sew up along the side edge. Create a cord in

Mulberry by cutting a length of yarn, folding it in half and twisting it tightly. Then fold it in half again and knot the end. Weave the cord in and out of the purse.

Strap
Using Crepe, cast on 20 sts.
Row 1: Purl.
Cast off and attach to the purse.

Miss Penelope Puss

Everybody loves the beach, especially Miss Penelope Puss. When those first rays of summer approach she's the first to the seaside and the last to leave when summer turns to autumn. She loves to laze around in the sun and splash away in the cool ocean. She's the perfect companion to take along on a seaside holiday. Just don't forget to pack the sun screen!

You will need

2 x 50 g (2 oz) balls Wendy Merino DK, Silver (DK, 100 per cent merino wool, 116 m per ball)

25 g (1 oz) ball Wendy Merino DK, Birch (DK, 100 per cent merino wool, 116 m per ball)

1 x 50 g (2 oz) ball Wendy Merino DK, Periwinkle (DK, 100 per cent merino wool, 116 m per ball)

1 x 50 g (2 oz) ball Wendy Merino DK, Cloud Dancer (DK, 100 per cent merino wool, 116 m per ball)

Small amount of Jet yarn for features

3.5 mm (US 4) knitting needles

Wool needle

Toy filling

Holding needle

Crochet hook

LEGS

(Make 2, working from sole.)

With Silver, cast on 22 sts.

Row 1 and all odd rows: Purl.

Row 2: K1, [kfb] 20 times, k1. 42 sts

Rows 3–17: Work in st st for 15 rows.

Row 18: K7, [k2tog] 14 times, k7. 28 sts

Row 19: Purl.

Row 20: K7, [k2tog] 7 times, k7. 21 sts

Rows 21–49: St st 29 rows.

Row 50: K4, [k2tog] twice, k5, [k2tog] twice, k4. 17 sts

Cast off loosely. Sew up the sole of the foot first and continue along the back edge, leaving the cast-off edge open. Stuff firmly.

ARMS

(Make 2.)

Starting from the top of the arms, cast on 8 sts in Silver.

Row 1: Kfb, k to the end. 9 sts

Row 2: Pfb, p to the end. 10 sts

Rows 3–4: Repeat the last 2 rows. 12 sts

Rows 5–6: Cast on 2 sts at the beginning of the next 2 rows. 16 sts

Rows 7–26: St st 20 rows.

Row 27: Change to Birch and k1, [kfb, k1] 7 times, k1. 23 sts.

Row 28: Purl.

Row 29: K1, [k1, kfb, k1] 7 times, k1. 30 sts

Rows 30–34: St st 5 rows.

Finger 1

Row 35: Cast off 3 sts, k10 and turn. Continue to work on these 10 sts, leaving the other 15 sts waiting.

Rows 36–38: St st 3 rows.

Row 39: *K2tog; rep from * to end. 5 sts

Break off yarn, thread yarn end through rem sts and fasten off.

Finger 2

Row 35: Cast on 3 sts, pick up the next 4 sts on needle and turn.

Row 36: Cast on 3 sts and work to end.

Rows 37–38: St st 2 rows.

Row 39: As above.

Finger 3

Pick up the next 10 sts on needle and work as follows:

Rows 35–38: St st 4 rows.

Row 39: *K2tog; rep from * to end. 5 sts

Join yarn to the last 3 sts and cast off.

Sew along the inside of all 3 fingers, then join the bottom of the second finger to the cast-off edge. Sew along the side of the arm, stuff and attach to the body.

BODY

Starting at neck, cast on 16 sts using Silver.

Rows 1–2: Work in st st beg with a k row.

Row 3: K1, [kfb] 14 times, k1. 30 sts

Rows 4–8: Work in st st for 5 rows.

Row 9: K1, [kfb] 28 times, k1. 58 sts

Rows 10–36: Work in st st for 27 rows.

Row 37: K1, [k2tog] 28 times, k1. 30 sts

Rows 38–42: Work in st st for 5 rows.

Row 43: K1, [k2tog] 14 times, k1. 16 sts

Break off yarn and draw yarn end through rem sts, pull tight and fasten off. Sew along the side and stuff before sewing up the neck edge.

HEAD

With Silver, cast on 15 sts.

Rows 1–2: St st 2 rows.

Row 3: K1, [kfb] 13 times, k1. 28 sts

Row 4 and all even rows: Purl.

Row 5: K1, [kfb, k1] 13 times, k1. 41 sts

Rows 6–8: Work in st st for 3 rows.

Row 9: K1, [k1, kfb, k1] 13 times, k1. 54 sts

Rows 10–14: Work in st st for 5 rows.

Row 15: K1, [k1, kfb, k2] 13 times, k1. 67 sts

Rows 16–30: Work in st st for 15 rows.

Row 31: K5, k2tog, [k7, k2tog] 6 times, k6. 60 sts

Row 32–36: St st 5 rows.

Row 37: K2, [k1, k2tog, k1] 14 times, k2. 46 sts

Rows 38–40: St st 3 rows.

Row 41: K2, [k1, k2tog] 14 times, k2. 32 sts

Rows 42–46: Change to Birch and st st.

Row 47: K1, [k2tog, k1] 10 times, k1. 22 sts

Row 49: K1, [k2tog] 10 times, k1. 12 sts

Break yarn off and thread yarn end through rem sts. Pull tight and fasten off. Sew up along the side of the muzzle and head, leaving a gap at the end for stuffing and adding facial features prior to closing up.

NOSE

In black, cast on 7 sts.

Rows 1–2: St st beg with a k row.

Row 3: K2tog, k3, k2tog. 5 sts

Row 4: P2tog, p1, p2tog. 3 sts

Row 5: K3tog.

Leaving a fairly long yarn end, cut yarn and pull through rem st. Attach to the front of the snout and using the

leftover thread embroider a smile by sewing a vertical line of back stitch downward and then creating a semi-circle for the mouth.

EARS

(Make 2)

In Silver, cast on 22 sts.

Rows 1–4: St st 4 rows.

Row 5: K4, [k2tog] twice, k6, [k2tog] twice, k4. 18 sts

Row 6 and all even rows: Purl.

Row 7: K3, [k2tog] twice, k4, [k2tog] twice, k3. 14 sts

Row 9: K2, [k2tog] twice, k2, [k2tog] twice, k2. 10 sts

Row 11: K1, [k2tog] 4 times, k1. 6 sts

Cast off and fold in half. Sew along the top and side edge and attach to each side of the head.

EYES

(Make 2.)

With Birch, cast on 5 sts.

Rows 1–4: St st beg with a k row.

Row 5: K2tog, k1, k2tog. 3 sts

Cast off.

For the pupil, chain 6 sts and join in a round. Attach to the centre of the eye, then fasten the eyes on each side of the head.

For the eyelashes unravel some black yarn and sew three curved lines of back stitches above each eye.

OUTFIT

BIKINI BOTTOMS

Starting from the bottom of the leg, cast on 30 sts in Periwinkle

Row 1–2: St st 2 rows.

Row 3–4: Change to Cloud Dancer and st st 2 rows.

(Continue to alternate these two colours every 2 rows.)

Row 5–6: St st 2 rows in Periwinkle. Leave the stitches on a spare needle and create a second identical piece.

Row 7: K30 and pick up and k the 30 sts waiting. 60 sts.

Row 8–20: St st 13 rows

Row 21: [K6, k2tog, k14, k2tog, k6] twice. 56 sts

Cast off tightly. Sew along the side edge and up the back.

BIKINI TOP

With Periwinkle, cast on 58 sts.

Rows 1–6: St st 6 rows, alternating Periwinkle and Cloud Dancer every 2 rows.

Row 7: Cast off 16 sts, k to end. 42 sts

Row 8: Cast off 16 sts, p to end. 26 sts

Row 9: K2tog, k9, k2tog. Turn and leave the remaining 13 sts on a spare needle. 11 sts

Row 10 and all even rows: Purl.

Row 11: K2tog, k7, k2tog. 9 sts

Row 13: K2tog, k5, k2tog. 7 sts

Row 15: K2tog, k3, k2tog. 5 sts

Rows 16–31: St st 16 rows.

Cast off and repeat rows 9–31 for remaining 13 sts. Attach the shoulder seams together and sew along the back edge.

SANDALS

With Periwinkle, cast on 10 sts.
Row 1: Kfb, k8, kfb. 12 sts
Row 2: Kfb, k10, kfb. 14 sts
Rows 3–26: Garter st (knit every row).
Row 27: K2tog, k10, k2tog. 12 sts
Row 28: K2tog, k8, k2tog. 10 sts
Cast off.

Strap

Using Cloud Dancer, cast on 30 sts.
Rows 1–6: St st 6 rows.
Row 7: Cast off 25 sts, k to end. 5 sts
Rows 8–26: St st 19 rows.
Cast off.
Attach the cast-on edge to the back of the sandal and attach the strap over the top.

BEACH BAG

Using Periwinkle, cast on 40 sts.
Rows 1–4: St st 4 rows.
Row 5: Change to Cloud Dancer and [k1, kfb, k16 , kfb, k1] twice. 44 sts
Rows 6–8: St st 3 rows.
Row 9: Change to Periwinkle and [k1, kfb, k18 , kfb, k1] twice. 48 sts
Rows 10–12: St st 3 rows.
Row 13: Change to Cloud Dancer and [k1, kfb, k20, kfb, k1] twice. 52 sts
Rows 14–16: St st 3 rows.
Row 17: Change to Periwinkle and [k1, kfb, k22 , kfb, k1] twice. 56 sts
Row 18: Purl.
Row 19: K12, cast off 6 sts, k20, cast off 6 sts, k12. 44 sts
Row 20: P12, cast on 16 sts, p20, cast on 16 sts, p12. 64 sts
Cast off and sew up along the side and base.

Projects

81

Miss Shirley Sheep

Miss Shirley Sheep is a very keen and eager pupil dressed in her smartest school uniform and ready for a day of learning. She has bought lovely new school shoes, which are embellished with cute little flowers and has her book bag in hand to carry all her school supplies.

You will need

1 x 50 g (2 oz) ball Wendy Merino DK, Birch (DK, 100 per cent merino wool, 116 m per ball)

1 x 50 g (2 oz) ball Wendy Merino DK, Wind Chime (DK, 100 per cent merino wool, 116 m per ball)

1 x 50 g (2 oz) ball Wendy Merino DK, Smoke (DK, 100 per cent merino wool, 116 m per ball)

1 x 50 g (2 oz) ball Wendy Merino DK, Cadet (DK, 100 per cent merino wool, 116 m per ball)

25 g (1 oz) ball Wendy Merino DK, Jet (DK, 100 per cent merino wool, 116 m per ball)

3.5 mm (US 4) knitting needles

Wool needle

Toy stuffing

Holding needle

2 small buttons

Cable needle

Crochet hook

LEGS

(Make 2, worked from sole.)

With Birch, cast on 22 sts.

Row 1 and all odd rows: Purl.

Row 2: K1, [kfb] 20 times, k1. 42 sts

Rows 3–17: Work in st st for 15 rows.

Row 18: K7, [k2tog] 14 times, k7. 28 sts

Row 20: K7, [k2tog] 7 times, k7. 21 sts

Rows 21–49: St st for 29 rows.

Row 50: K4, [k2tog] twice, k5, [k2tog] twice, k4. 17 sts

Cast off loosely. Sew up the sole first and continue along the back edge, leaving the cast-off edge open. Stuff firmly.

ARMS

Starting from the top of the arms, with Birch, cast on 8 sts.

Row 1: Kfb, knit to the end. 9 sts

Row 2: Pfb, purl to the end. 10 sts

Rows 3–4: Repeat the last 2 rows. 12 sts

Rows 5–6: Cast on 2 sts at the beginning of the next 2 rows. 16 sts

Rows 7–26: St st 20 rows.

Rows 27–30: Change to Wind Chime and st st 4 rows.

Row 31: K3, k2tog, k3 and turn. Work on these 7 sts and leave the other 8 sts on a holding needle.

Row 33: K2, k2tog, k3. 6 sts

Row 34 and 36: P.

Row 35: K2, k2tog, k2. 5 sts

Row 37: K1, k2tog, k2. 4 sts

Cast off and repeat the last 7 rows with the other 8 sts. Sew along the inside of the hoof and up the arm. Stuff firmly and attach to each side of the body.

BODY

(Make 1, starting at neck.)

With Birch, cast on 16 sts.

Rows 1–2: Work in st st for 2 rows.

Row 3: K1, [kfb] 14 times, k1. 30 sts

Rows 4–8: Work in st st.

Row 9: K1, [kfb] 28 times, k1. 58 sts

Rows 10–36: Work in st st.

Amigurumi Friends

Row 37: K1, [k2tog] 28 times, k1. 30 sts
Rows 38–42: Work in st st.
Row 43: K1, [k2tog] 14 times, k1. 16 sts
Break off yarn and draw yarn end through rem sts, pull tight and fasten off. Sew up along the side edge using mattress st and stuff when three-quarters stitched. Continue to the cast-on edge, then draw the yarn through the cast-on edge and pull tight. Fasten and secure any loose threads.

HEAD

With Birch, cast on 15 sts.
Rows 1–2: St st 2 rows.
Row 3: K1, [kfb] 13 times, k1. 28 sts
Row 4 and all even rows: Purl.
Row 5: K1, [kfb, k1] 13 times, k1. 41 sts
Rows 6–8: Work in st st.
Row 9: K1, [k1, kfb, k1] 13 times, k1. 54 sts
Rows 10–14: Work in st st.
Row 15: K1, [k1, kfb, k2] 13 times, k1. 67 sts
Rows 16–26: Work in st st for 11 rows, changing to Wind Chime at row 21.
Row 27: K3, [k2, k2tog, k2] 10 times, k4. 57 sts
Rows 28–32: St st 5 rows.
Row 33: K3, [k1, k2tog, k2] 10 times, k4. 47 sts
Rows 34–36: St st 3 rows.
Row 37: K3, [k1, k2tog, k1] 10 times, k4. 37 sts
Row 39: K3, [k2tog, k1] 10 times, k4. 27 sts
Row 41: K3, [k2tog] 10 times, k4. 17 sts
Row 42: P1, [p2tog] 8 times. 9 sts
Break yarn and draw yarn end through rem sts, pull tight and fasten off. Use mattress stitch to sew along the side edge. Stuff and add facial features prior to closing up.

EYES

(Make 2.)
With Birch, cast on 5 sts.
Rows 1–4: St st 4 rows.
Row 5: K2tog, k1, k2tog. 3 sts
Cast off.
For the pupil chain 6 sts and join in a round. Attach to the centre of the eye, then fasten the eyes on each side of the head.
For the eyelashes unravel some black yarn and sew three curved lines of back stitches above each eye.

EARS

(Make 2.)
With Birch, cast on 22 sts.
Rows 1–4: St st 4 rows.
Row 5: K2tog, k7, [k2tog] twice, k7, k2tog. 18 sts
Row 6: Purl.
Row 7: K2tog, k5, [k2tog] twice, k5, k2tog. 14 sts
Row 8: [P2tog] 7 times. 7 sts
Break yarn and thread yarn end through remaining stitches. Sew up along the top and side edge and attach to each side of the head.
For the snout, using the remaining yarn, sew a V-shape in back stitch at the front of the face, then add a vertical line downward and then create a semi-circle for the smile.

OUTFIT

SKIRT

With Smoke, cast on 122 sts.
Row 1: K3, [p4, k4] 14 times, p4, k3
Row 2: P3, k4, [p4, k4] 14 times, p3.
Rows 3–20: Repeat rows 1 and 2 nine times.
Row 21: K1, [place the next 2 sts on a cable needle and bring it to the front. Knit the first st on the cable and the next sts on the cable needle together. Repeat with the second st. Take the next 2 sts on the cable needle and bring them to the back. Knit the first st on the needle and the first st on the cable needle together. Repeat with the second sts] 15 times, k1. 62 sts
Rows 22–24: St st 3 rows.
Row 25: K1, [k7, k2tog, k6] 4 times, k1. 58 sts
Cast off and sew along the edge.

VEST

Starting from the rib of the vest, cast on 60 sts in Cadet.

Rows 1–6: Rib st 6 rows (k2, p2, starting with p1).

Rows 7–19: St st beg with a knit row.

Leave the first 45 sts on a holding needle and work on the left-hand 15 sts as follows:

Row 20: Purl.

Row 21: [k2tog] twice, k11. 13 sts

Row 23: [k2tog] twice, k9. 11 sts

Rows 24–27: St st 4 rows.

Row 28: Cast off 5 sts, p to end. 6 sts

Rows 29–30: St st 2 rows.

Cast off.

Join yarn to the central 30 sts on the purl side and work as follows:

Row 20: [P2tog] twice, p to end. 28 sts

Row 21: [k2tog] twice, k to end. 26 sts

Rows 22–23: Repeat rows 20–21. 22 sts

Rows 24–27: St st 4 rows.

Row 28: P6, cast off 10 sts, p6.

Rows 29–30: St st 2 rows.

Cast off.

Repeat rows 29–30 for the 6 sts on the other side.

Join yarn to the last 15 sts and work as follows:

Row 20: [P2tog] twice, p to end. 13 sts

Row 21: Knit.

Row 22–23: Repeat rows 26 and 27. 11 sts

Row 24–26: St st.

Row 27: Cast off 5 sts, k6. 6 sts

Rows 28–30: St st 3 rows.

Cast off. Use mattress stitch to sew along the back edge and across the shoulders.

SLEEVES

(Make 2.)

With Cloud Dancer, cast on 24 sts.

Rows 1–6: St st 6 rows.

Rows 7–12: Cast off 3 sts at the beginning of the next 6 rows. 6 sts

Cast off.

Sew the sides of the sleeves and attach to the jumper.

COLLAR

With Cloud Dancer, cast on 50 sts.

Rows 1–2: St st.

Row 3: [k4, k2tog, k4] 5 times. 45 sts

Cast off tightly. Attach the cast-off edge to the neck of the vest.

SHOES

(Make 2.)

With Jet, cast on 24 sts.

Row 1 and all odd rows: Purl.

Row 2: K1, [kfb] 22 times, k1. 46 sts

Rows 3–17: Work in st st for 15 rows.

Row 18: K8, [k2tog] 15 times, k8. 31 sts

Cast off and sew along the heel and side.

SATCHEL

(Make 2.)

Using Cadet, cast on 20 sts.

Rows 1–36: St st 36 rows.

Row 37: K1, k2tog, yo, k14, yo, k2tog, k1.

Row 38: Purl.

Cast off and fold over. Sew along the side edge and add 2 buttons level with the eyelets.

Strap

Using Cadet, cast on 14 sts.

Row 1: K.

Cast off and stitch to the top of the satchel.

Miss Suzy Squirrel

Miss Suzy Squirrel is not much of a morning person, nor is she an evening person. Her favourite activities include sleeping, lazing around and cuddling up with her teddy and hot water bottle. Her onesie even has a convenient little pouch to carry these accessories or could even hold an evening snack when she goes fridge-raiding in her bunny slippers!

You will need

2 x 50 g (2 oz) balls Wendy Merino DK, Spice (DK, 100 per cent merino wool, 116 m per ball)

1 x 50 g (2 oz) ball Wendy Merino DK, Cloud Dancer (DK, 100 per cent merino wool, 116 m per ball)

1 x 50 g (2 oz) ball Wendy Merino DK, Seaspray (DK, 100 per cent merino wool, 116 m per ball)

1 x 50 g (2 oz) ball Wendy Merino DK, Watermelon (DK, 100 per cent merino wool, 116 m per ball)

A small amount of Jet yarn

3.5 mm (US 4) knitting needles

Wool needle

Toy stuffing

Holding needle

Crochet hook

LEGS

(Make 2, working from the sole.)

With Spice, cast on 22 sts.

Row 1 and all odd rows: Purl.

Row 2: K1, [kfb] 20 times, k1. 42 sts

Rows 3–17: Work in st st for 15 rows.

Row 18: K7, [k2tog] 14 times, k7. 28 sts

Row 20: K7, [k2tog] 7 times, k7. 21 sts

Rows 21–49: Work in st st for 29 rows.

Row 50: K4, [k2tog] twice, k5, [k2tog] twice, k4. 17 sts

Cast off loosely. Sew up the bottom of the foot first and continue along the back edge, leaving the cast-off edge open. Stuff firmly.

ARMS

(Make 2.)

Starting from the top of the arms, cast on 8 sts in Spice.

Row 1: Kfb1, k to the end. 9 sts

Row 2: Pfb1, p to the end. 10 sts

Rows 3–4: Repeat rows 1 and 2. 12 sts

Rows 5–6: Cast on 2 sts at the beginning of the next 2 rows. 16 sts

Rows 7–26: St st.

Rows 27–28: Change to Birch and st st 2 rows.

Row 29: Cast off the first 3 sts and then work as follows for the fingers:

Finger 1

Row 29: [Kfb] 3 times, turn. 6 sts

Rows 30–32: St st 3 rows.

Row 33: [K2tog] 3 times. 3 sts

Break yarn and thread yarn end through the 3 remaining sts. Pull tight and fasten. Sew along the edge of the finger.

Finger 2

Join the yarn to the next 2 sts and knit as follows:

Row 29: Cast on 2 sts, k to end. 4 sts

Row 30: Cast on 2 sts, p to end. 6 sts

Row 31–32: St st 2 rows.

Row 33: [K2tog] 3 times. 3 sts

Break yarn and thread through the remaining sts. Pull tight and fasten off. Sew along the edge of the finger.
Repeat finger 2 and finger 1, then cast off the remaining 3 sts. Attach the cast-off edge to the bottom of fingers 2 and 3, then sew up along the side of the arm and stuff firmly.

BODY

(Make 1, starting at neck.)
With Spice, cast on 16 sts.
Rows 1–2: Work in st st, beg with a knit row.
Row 3: K1, [kfb] 14 times, k1. 30 sts
Rows 4–8: Work in st st beg with a purl row.
Row 9: K1, [kfb] 28 times, k1. 58 sts
Rows 10–36: Work in st st for 27 rows.
Row 37: K1, [k2tog] 28 times, k1. 30 sts
Rows 38–42: Work in st st for 5 rows.
Row 43: K1, [k2tog] 14 times, k1. 16 sts
Break yarn and thread yarn end through rem sts, pull tight and fasten off. Sew up along the side edge using mattress st and stuff when three-quarters stitched. Continue to the cast-on edge, then draw the yarn through the cast-on edge and pull tight. Fasten and secure any loose threads.

HEAD

With Spice, cast on 15 sts.
Rows 1–2: St st, beg with a knit row.
Row 3: K1, [kfb] 13 times, k1. 28 sts
Row 4 and all even rows: Purl.
Row 5: K1, [kfb, k1] 13 times, k1. 41 sts
Rows 6–8: Work in st st for 3 rows.
Row 9: K1, [k1, kfb, k1] 13 times, k1. 54 sts
Rows 10–14: Work in st st for 5 rows.
Row 15: K1, [k1, kfb, k2] 13 times, k1. 67 sts
Rows 16–30: Work in st st for 15 rows.
Row 31: K10 [k2tog] 6 times, k21, [k2tog] 7 times, k10. 54 sts
Rows 32–36: St st 5 rows.
Row 37: K7, [k2tog] 6 times, k14, [k2tog] 7 times, k7. 41 sts

Row 38–40: St st 3 rows.
Row 41: K3, [k2tog] 6 times, k8, [k2tog] 7 times, k4. 28 sts
Rows 42–44: St st 3 rows.
Row 45: K3, [k2tog] 4 times, k6, [k2tog] 4 times, k3. 20 sts
Row 47: K2, [k2tog] 3 times, k4, [k2tog] 3 times, k2. 14 sts
Row 49: K1, [k2tog] 2 times, k3, [k2tog] 2 times, k2. 10 sts
Cast off.
Use mattress stitch to sew along the side edge. Stuff and add facial features before closing.

NOSE

Cast on 9 sts in Jet.
Rows 1–2: St st 2 rows.
Row 3: K2tog, k5, k2tog. 7 sts
Row 4 and all even rows: P.
Row 5: K2tog, k3, k2tog. 5 sts
Row 6: K2tog, k1, k2tog. 3 sts
Cast off leaving a long tail. Attach the nose to the front of the face using running stitches, then with the remaining yarn, use running stitch to embroider a vertical line for approximately 2 cm (¾ in), then a semi-circle for the smile. Use the running stitch to fill in the gaps between the stitches.

EARS

(Make 2.)
Cast on 22 sts in Spice
Rows 1–6: St st 6 rows.
Row 7: Change to Cloud Dancer and work as follows: K4, [k2tog] twice, k6, [k2tog] twice, k4. 18 sts
Row 8 and all even rows: Purl.
Row 9: K3, [k2tog] twice, k4, [k2tog] twice, k3. 14 sts
Row 11: K2, [k2tog] twice, k2, [k2tog] twice, k2. 10 sts
Row 13: K1, [k2tog] 4 times, k1. 6 sts
Cast off and fold in half. Sew along the top and side edge and attach to each side of the head.

EYES

(Make 2.)
With Cloud Dancer, cast on 5 sts.

Rows 1–4: St st 4 rows.
Row 5: K2tog, k1, k2tog. 3 sts Cast off.
For the pupil, chain 6 sts and join in a round. Attach to the centre of the eye, then fasten the eyes on each side of the head.
For the eyelashes, unravel some black yarn and sew three curved lines of back stitches above each eye.

OUTFIT

ONESIE
Starting from the bottom of the leg, cast on 24 sts in Seaspray.
Row 1: [Kfb, k1] 12 times. 36 sts
Rows 2–4: St st 3 rows.
Row 5: [K2, kfb, k3] 6 times. 42 sts
Rows 6–24: St st 19 rows.
Break off yarn and place the remaining sts on a holding needle. Knit an identical trouser leg.
Row 25: K42 sts and pick up and knit the 42 sts from the holding needle. 84 sts
Rows 26–40: St st 15 rows.
Row 41: K2, [k3, k2tog, k3] 10 times, k2. 74 sts
Rows 42–54: St st 14 rows.
Row 55: K17, cast off 4 sts, k32, cast off 4 sts, k17.
Leave the first 17 and middle 32 sts on a holding needle and work on the left-hand 17 sts as follows:
Row 56 and all even rows: Purl.
Row 57: [k2tog] twice, k13. 15 sts
Row 58: Purl.
Row 59: [k2tog] twice, k11. 13 sts
Rows 60–63: St st 4 rows.
Row 64: Cast off 6 sts, k7. 7 sts
Row 65–66: St st 2 rows.
Cast off.
Join yarn to the 32 sts waiting on purl side and work as follows:
Row 56: [P2tog] twice, p to end. 30 sts
Row 57: [k2tog] twice, k to end. 28 sts

Rows 58–59: Repeat rows 56 and 57. 24 sts
Rows 60–63: St st 4 rows.
Row 64: P7, cast off 10 sts, p7.
Rows 65–66: St st 2 rows.
Cast off.
Repeat rows 64–66 for the 7 sts on the other side.
Join yarn to the last 17 sts waiting and work as follows:
Row 56: [P2tog] twice, p to end. 15 sts
Row 57: Knit.
Rows 58–59: Repeat rows 56 and 57. 13 sts
Rows 60–62: St st 3 rows.
Row 63: Cast off 6 sts, k7. 7 sts.
Rows 64–66: St st 3 rows.
Cast off.

SLEEVES
(Make 2.)
Starting from the cuff, cast on 20 sts in Seaspray.
Rows 2–4: St st 3 rows.
Row 5: [K2, kfb, k3] 5 times. 35 sts
Rows 6–18: St st 13 rows.
Rows 19–24: Cast off 5 sts at the beginning of the next 6 rows and work to the end. 5 sts
Cast off. Sew along the side of the legs and the back of the sleepsuit. Sew up the side edge of the sleeves and attach to the armholes.

POCKET
Cast on 22 sts in Watermelon.
Rows 1–6: Work in k2, p2 rib.
Rows 7–16: St st 10 rows.
Cast off and sew onto the front of the sleepsuit.

SLIPPERS
With Seaspray, cast on 26 sts.
Row 1 and all odd rows: Purl.
Row 2: K1, [kfb] 24 times, k1. 50 sts
Rows 3–17: Work in st st for 15 rows.
Row 18: K8, [k2tog] 17 times, k8. 33 sts
Cast off. Sew along the sole and the side of the slipper.

Slipper ears
Cast on 16 sts in Watermelon.
Rows 1–10: St st 10 rows.
Row 11: [K2tog] 8 times. 8 sts.
Break off yarn and thread through rem sts. Fold the ears
in half and sew up the edge. Use Seaspray to add facial
features.
For the eyes, add two small stitches on each side of the face
for the eyes, then use satin stitch to embroider a triangle for
the nose.

DOG'S LEGS
(Make 4.)
Cast on 12 sts in Cloud Dancer.
Rows 1–8: St st 8 rows.
Row 9: [K2tog] 6 times. 6 sts
Break yarn and thread through remaining sts. Sew along the
side edge.

DOG'S BODY AND HEAD
Cast on 10 sts in Cloud Dancer.
Row 1: [Kfb] 10 times. 20 sts
Rows 2–10: St st 9 rows.
Row 11: [K2tog] 10 times. 10 sts
Row 12 and all even rows: Purl.
Row 13: [Kfb] 10 times. 20 sts
Row 15: [Kfb, k1] 10 times. 30 sts
Rows 16–22: St st 7 rows.
Row 23: [K2tog, k1] 10 times. 20 sts
Row 24: [P2tog] 10 times. 10 sts
Break off yarn and thread yarn end through remaining sts.
Sew up the back edge and stuff firmly. Add facial features
before closing and attach legs and arms.
For the eyes, use a small amount of Seaspray and add two
small stitches on each side of the face for the eyes, then use
satin stitch to embroider a triangle for the nose.

DOG'S EARS
Cast on 6 sts in Cloud Dancer.
Rows 1–8: St st beg with a knit row.
Row 9: K2tog, k2, k2tog. 4 sts Cast off and attach to the
dog's head.

HOT WATER BOTTLE
Cast on 22 sts in Watermelon.
Rows 1–12: St st 12 rows.
Row 13: [K2tog] twice, k3, [k2tog] 4 times, k3, [K2tog]
twice. 14 sts
Row 14: P2tog, p3, [p2tog] twice, p3, p2tog. 10 sts
Row 15: K2tog, k1, [k2tog] twice, k1, k2tog. 6 sts
Rows 16–18: St st 3 rows.
Row 19: [K2tog] 6 times. 12 sts
Cast off and sew along the bottom and side edge. Stuff
slightly and close by adding a few sts to the top. Leave the
cast-off edge open.

Acknowledgements

To Craig, my ever-patient husband, I may not always appear to appreciate your feedback but usually end up changing the flaws you've pointed out.

A great big thank you goes to my two amazing little boys who are a constant source of inspiration with their imaginative suggestions. Your smiles and giggles brighten up my life and make the sleepless nights worthwhile.

Thank you to Simona Hill, Diana Ward and Lliane Clarke at New Holland Publishers for your support and guidance and the lovely Carolann Allen at TB Ramsden for so generously providing the yarn for this project.

Last, but not least, a huge thank you goes to my amazingly efficient test knitters: Diane Elliott, Glenda Parsons and Giovanna Beier, who unpicked and improved many of my patterns.